IRON WILL STEEL PHYSIQUE

IRON WILL STEEL PHYSIQUE

MACK RAFEAL

Noble Publishing

CONTENTS

INDEX	1
Introduction	3
Chapter 1	8
Chapter 2	25
Chapter 3	41
Chapter 4	58
Chapter 5	74
Chapter 6	92
Chapter 7	108
Chapter 8	123
Chapter 9	138

INDEX

Introduction

Chapter 1: The Genesis of Iron Will
1.1 Introduction to the concept of developing mental resilience and determination
1.2 Personal stories of individuals who overcame obstacles through sheer willpower
1.3 Establishing the connection between mental strength and physical transformation

Chapter 2: Forging the Mind: The Mental Blueprint
2.1 Exploring the psychology of discipline and focus
2.2 Techniques for developing a strong mindset for fitness goals
2.3 Setting realistic expectations and cultivating a positive mental attitude

Chapter 3: The Anvil of Discipline
3.1 Understanding the role of discipline in building a steel physique
3.2 Strategies for creating and maintaining healthy habits
3.3 Overcoming common challenges and temptations

Chapter 4: Hammering Out Goals
4.1 Setting SMART goals for physical fitness
4.2 Creating a personalized workout and nutrition plan
4.3 Tracking progress and making adjustments along the way

Chapter 5: The Furnace of Resilience
5.1 Resilience as a key factor in overcoming setbacks
5.2 Strategies for bouncing back from injuries or setbacks
5.3 Learning from failures and turning them into opportunities for growth

Chapter 6: Sculpting the Body: Training Techniques
6.1 Introduction to different workout routines for strength and muscle building
6.2 Incorporating variety and intensity into training sessions
6.3 Balancing cardiovascular exercise with strength training

Chapter 7: Fueling the Fire: Nutrition for Strength
7.1 The importance of a balanced and nutritious diet in achieving fitness goals
7.2 Tailoring nutrition to support muscle growth and recovery
7.3 Dispelling common myths about diet and fitness

Chapter 8: The Crucible of Endurance
8.1 Exploring the role of endurance in physical fitness
8.2 Strategies for building cardiovascular stamina
8.3 Cross-training and its benefits for overall fitness

Chapter 9: Forged in Steel: Achieving Lasting Transformation
9.1 Celebrating success stories of individuals who have transformed their bodies and lives
9.2 Emphasizing the ongoing nature of personal development and fitness
9.3 Encouraging readers to continue refining both their iron will and steel physique

Introduction

In the tremendous embroidery of human life, certain people rise up out of the cauldron of existence with an unmatched assurance that separates them — a versatility that rises above the common and boundaries on the unprecedented. Such figures become living demonstrations of the unstoppable force of the human soul, manufacturing their fates with an iron will and chiseling their builds with a relentless strength that challenges the limitations of difficulty. It is inside this domain of enduring purpose and imposing flexibility that we dig into the convincing account of "Iron Will, Steel Build."

At its center, this investigation is an excursion into the profundities of human potential — the convergence of mental backbone and actual ability. An odyssey welcomes us to disentangle the narratives of people who, despite everything, developed an iron will that filled in as the bedrock for the development of a steel physical make-up. This entwining of psyche and body winds around a story embroidery that stretches across societies, periods, and various scenes, offering significant bits of knowledge into the human condition.

In the pages that follow, we will set out on a journey through the chronicles of history, investigating the existences of notorious figures whose stories resound with the reverberations of assurance and strength. From old champions who shaped their bodies through thorough preparation to cutting edge competitors who resist the limits of human potential, every story adds to the aggregate account of the unstoppable soul that impels mankind forward.

The idea of an "iron will" is established in the possibility of a tough purpose — an enduring assurance that drives forward even with affliction. A psychological steadiness will not surrender to the difficulties and hindrances that life presents. The term invokes pictures of flexibility, coarseness, and an undaunted obligation to one's objectives. Whether in the war zone of old history or the fields of current games, the sign of an iron will has been a main thrust behind momentous human accomplishments.

At the same time, the idea of a "steel body" addresses the actual sign of this unflinching outlook. It is a demonstration of the extraordinary force of restrained preparing, pushing the limits of the human body to accomplish accomplishments that appear to be godlike. The steel physical make-up isn't only a presentation of muscle and ligament however a living demonstration of the cooperative energy among psyche and body, mirroring an agreeable equilibrium that raises human potential to remarkable levels.

To comprehend the beginning of such surprising people, we should turn our look to the cauldron of their encounters — the minutes that tried their strength and the pots that fashioned their unwavering purpose.

The pages of history are packed with stories of heroes, researchers, and competitors who, through an intermingling of situation and individual decision, tackled the force of an iron will to shape a steel body.

Old civic establishments give a rich embroidery of such stories, with incredible champions and thinkers encapsulating the goals of mental grit and actual ability. In the blessed corridors of old Greece, the idea of arete, a prudence enveloping greatness in both psyche and body, turned into a core value for people trying to rise above their limits. Any semblance of Leonidas, the Austere ruler, and Milo of Croton, the prestigious grappler, arose as paragons of this all encompassing way to deal with human potential.

Leonidas, deified for his administration in the Skirmish of Thermopylae, encapsulated the Simple ethos of discipline and generosity. His iron will, produced through the requesting agoge preparing from youth, empowered him to stand fearless against overpowering chances. The Spartans accepted that a sound brain dwelled in a sound body, and Leonidas represented this conviction with his powerful build and unshakeable purpose.

Likewise, Milo of Croton's story reverberates through the ages as a demonstration of the extraordinary force of predictable, demanding preparation. The prestigious grappler's unbelievable accomplishments, for example, conveying a developing calf on his shoulders day to day, displayed his tremendous actual strength as well as the psychological discipline expected to support such undertakings. Milo's quest for greatness in both mental and actual domains fills in as a worldview for those seeking to develop an iron will and a steel physical make-up.

As the embroidery of time unfurls, the archaic period acquaints us with knights and champions whose lives were molded by the cauldron of fighting. During a time where actual ability frequently resolved endurance, knights epitomized the combination of military expertise and relentless purpose. The middle age code of valor, with its accentuation on honor, devotion, and boldness, turned into the pot where the steel physical make-ups of knights were tempered.

One can't retell the stories of archaic courage without conjuring the incredible figure of Richard the Lionheart. A fighter ruler whose missions during the Third Campaign made a permanent imprint on history, Richard exemplified the chivalric ideal of a respectable champion. His endeavors on the war zone, combined with a build sharpened through thorough preparation, displayed the cooperative connection between the iron will to overcome difficulty and the steel physical make-up that could endure the afflictions of middle age battle.

The Renaissance time frame, set apart by a resurgence of interest in traditional beliefs, saw the rise of polymaths who encapsulated the marriage of scholarly discernment and actual ability.

Figures like Leonardo da Vinci and Michelangelo, while celebrated for their imaginative virtuoso, were additionally models of people whose trained lives mirrored the amalgamation of brain and body.

Leonardo da Vinci, frequently venerated for his magnum opuses like the Mona Lisa and The Last Dinner, was not simply a painter but rather a polymath whose interests crossed life systems, designing, and actual wellness. His scratch pad are packed with representations of the human body, mirroring a sharp interest in the exchange among muscles and development. Leonardo's all encompassing way to deal with the human structure highlights the conviction that a developed brain should track down articulation through a vigorous and coordinated constitution.

In the mean time, Michelangelo, the stone worker of notable works like the Sculpture of David, epitomized the Renaissance ideal of the total person. His devotion to the flawlessness of structure and extent in his figures reflected a promise to actual greatness. Michelangelo's etched manifestations appeared to rise out of the stone with an imperativeness that repeated the stone worker's own focused way to deal with both mental and actual pursuits.

The period of investigation and colonization introduced another time of difficulties and open doors, testing the strength of people who wandered into the unexplored world. Pilgrims and globe-trotters, driven by a voracious interest and a really considering spiriting, explored strange waters and overcame cold scenes. Their stories reverberate with the unstoppable will that impelled them to overcome the physical and mental difficulties experienced on their excursions.

Sir Ernest Shackleton's disastrous campaign to Antarctica fills in as a piercing illustration of versatility despite outrageous misfortune. At the point when his boat, the Perseverance, became caught in the ice, Shackleton's authority and enduring assurance turned into the signal that directed his team through unfathomable difficulties. The experience requested actual perseverance as well as a psychological mettle that rose above the constraints of human strength. Shackleton's iron will, combined with the steel bodies of his group, guaranteed their endurance despite everything.

As the modern upheaval changed social orders and introduced a period of mechanical progression, the nexus between mental guts and actual ability tracked down new articulations. Trailblazers of industry and creators, driven by a dream of progress, explored strange domains in the domain of science and development. Their accounts uncover the cooperative connection between a relentless determination to conquer difficulties and the actual endurance expected to carry weighty plans to completion.

Thomas Edison, the productive creator whose manifestations enlightened the world, was a virtuoso of the psyche as well as a man of tenacious hard working attitude. His incalculable long periods of trial and error and enthusiastic quest for development requested scholarly splendor as well as the actual perseverance to support such undertakings.

Edison's life embodies the combination of an iron will to continue on through disappointments and misfortunes with a steel build equipped for persevering through the afflictions of eager work.

In the cauldron of the twentieth 100 years, the world saw the development of people whose accounts rose above public limits and social partitions. The domain of sports, specifically, turned into a phase where competitors displayed the unimaginable capability of the human body when pushed by a resolute assurance. From the boxing rings to the olympic style sports fields, competitors like Muhammad Ali and Jesse Owens scratched their names into history, leaving a persevering through tradition of iron will and steel build.

Muhammad Ali, known as "The Best," rose above the game of boxing to turn into a worldwide symbol of flexibility and conviction. His fights inside and outside the ring reflected the battles of society at large, and Ali's unfaltering obligation to his standards displayed an iron will that would not be broken. The actual ability he showed in the boxing ring, described by speed, nimbleness, and perseverance, was a demonstration of the agreeable connection between mental mettle and actual greatness.

Jesse Owens, the olympic style sports legend whose accomplishments at the 1936 Berlin Olympics opposed the bigoted belief systems of the time, epitomized the victory of the human soul over affliction. Owens' athletic ability, set apart by record-breaking exhibitions notwithstanding segregation, displayed the groundbreaking force of an iron will. His accomplishments were a triumph for himself as well as an emblematic victory of the human potential to beat obstructions through an unflinching mentality and a finely tuned physical make-up.

The post-war time saw the intermingling of international pressures and the journey for human investigation past Earth's limits. Space explorers, the trailblazers of room investigation, left on unsafe excursions that requested logical discernment as well as the psychological versatility to stand up to the unexplored world. The space race turned into a theater where people like Yuri Gagarin and Neil Armstrong showed the combination of an iron will with the actual ability expected to wander past the limits of our planet.

Yuri Gagarin, the principal human to circle the Earth, represented the victory of human resourcefulness and mental fortitude. His excursion into space required specialized mastery as well as the psychological guts to endure the physical and mental difficulties of room travel. Gagarin's heritage rose above public limits, filling in as a demonstration of the general desires of mankind to investigate the universe.

Neil Armstrong, the primary human to go to the moon, carved his name in history as a trailblazer of room investigation.

The Apollo 11 mission requested careful preparation and specialized aptitude, however it was Armstrong's quiet disposition and undaunted outlook that directed mankind through the memorable second. The steel build expected to explore the brutal lunar scene reflected the unstoppable soul that energized Armstrong's excursion to the moon.

As we explore the intricacies of the advanced time, the crossing point of innovation, science, and human likely keeps on reclassifying the limits of what is attainable. Pioneers and visionaries in fields going from business to medical care represent the combination of smartness and actual flexibility expected to explore the difficulties of the 21st hundred years. Figures like Elon Musk, known for his endeavors in space investigation and electric vehicles, epitomize the soul of present day pioneers pushing the envelope of probability.

Elon Musk, the business person and pioneer behind organizations like SpaceX and Tesla, has reshaped enterprises with his brassy vision. Musk's tenacious quest for aggressive objectives requires scholarly splendor as well as the actual endurance to support the requests of driving different notable endeavors all the while. His life fills in as a contemporary outline of the cooperative connection between an iron will to imagine the future and a steel build equipped for understanding those dreams.

In the different embroidery of mankind's set of experiences, the story of "Iron Will, Steel Physical make-up" arises as a demonstration of the persevering through characteristics that push people to rise above their limits. From old champions to current trailblazers, the accounts woven into this investigation enlighten the significant exchange between mental mettle and actual ability. The iron will that endured everyday hardship and the steel constitution that bore the engravings of flexibility allure us to think about our own ability for development and change.

In the sections that follow, we will dig further into the existences of people who, through the pot of their encounters, epitomized the goals of an iron will and a steel constitution. Their accounts, set apart by wins and afflictions, offer significant experiences into the human condition and the unlimited potential that dwells inside every one of us. As we set out on this odyssey through time and across different scenes, the strings of assurance, discipline, and strength will wind around a story that rises above ages and motivates us to go after new levels of human accomplishment.

Chapter 1

The Genesis of Iron Will

In the chronicles of mankind's set of experiences, there exists an embroidery woven with the strings of versatility, assurance, and unfaltering determination. A story rises above time, a story that unfurls across ages, forming fates and embellishment the course of civilizations. This adventure, carved in the texture of our reality, is, as a matter of fact, the beginning of Iron Will — a power that rises up out of the pot of difficulty, producing unyielding spirits fit for enduring the most imposing difficulties.

The story starts in the cauldron of individual battles, where common people end up went up against by the brutal real factors of life. These are the minutes when the human soul is tried, when the courage of one's personality is fashioned in the flames of difficulty. It is inside this cauldron that the seeds of Iron Will are planted, flourishing in the ripe soil of assurance.

Think about the story of a youthful craftsman, working in haziness, wrestling with self-question and cultural assumptions. The material of their life is clear, and the brush of predetermination floats uncertainly over the range of conceivable outcomes. However, inside the profundities of their being, a flash lights — an ash of energy that won't be quenched. This is the undeveloped phase of Iron Will, where the individual faces the overwhelming assignment of cutting their own way, regardless of the snags that substitute their direction.

As the story unfurls, we cross ages and witness the development of Iron Will from an individualistic idea to an aggregate power that shapes the fate of networks and countries. A power drives social orders forward, even despite unrealistic chances. The reverberations of Iron Will resound in the narratives of civic establishments, from the ascent of domains to the fall of traditions.

Consider the flexibility of a country rising up out of the remains of contention, revamping itself with an assurance that outperforms the scars of war. The residents, battered and wounded, stand joined in their determination to outline another course. This aggregate Iron Will turns into the bedrock whereupon the groundworks of a reestablished society are laid. The paste ties unique components into a strong entire, a power that changes misfortune into a potential open door.

In the fabulous woven artwork of mankind's set of experiences, there are critical minutes where the beginning of Iron Will is exposed for all to observe. One such age is the battle for social equality, where people from underestimated networks rose against the tide of abuse. The social liberties development turns into a cauldron, testing the determination of the individuals who really hoped for balance and equity. Notwithstanding fundamental separation, these people called the strength of Iron Will to destroy the shackles of bias and fashion a way towards a more comprehensive society.

The adventure of Iron Will isn't restricted to the great phase of authentic occasions alone; it pervades the actual texture of regular day to day existence. Think about the narrative of a solitary parent, shuffling the obligations of work and family, confronting misfortune with a steely assurance. This regular legend encapsulates the substance of Iron Will, exploring the difficulties of existence with beauty and backbone. It is in the little, apparently subtle minutes that the genuine courage of Iron Will is uncovered.

As the account unfurls, we dive into the domains of science and advancement, where trailblazers and visionaries resist the constraints of human information. The journey for information itself turns into a demonstration of the persevering quest for progress, driven by an unquenchable interest and a steadfast assurance to disentangle the secrets of the universe. The beginning of Iron Will in the logical area is described by the unstoppable soul to push the limits of what is known and investigate the unfamiliar regions of human comprehension.

In the cauldron of investigation, space explorers set out on hazardous excursions into the universe, confronting the tremendousness of room with a fortitude that rises above natural limits. The space race turns into a sign of aggregate Iron Will, as countries contend not only for incomparability but rather for the progression of human potential. The difficulties of room travel are met with development and resolve, as mankind extends its cutoff points to contact the stars.

The story turns to the domain of business venture, where visionaries hope against hope past the bounds of show. The beginning of Iron Will in the enterprising scene is set apart by the dauntlessness to rock the boat and the constancy to face the hardships of vulnerability. Business people, furnished with a dream and powered by an energy, explore the turbulent oceans of business with a faithful obligation to see their fantasies emerge.

Think about the narrative of a beginning up organizer, wrestling with the vulnerabilities of an unpredictable market. Even with mishaps and cynics, the business visionary depends on the wellspring of Iron Will to endure. This strength changes simple thoughts into progressive advancements, moving businesses forward and reshaping the monetary scene.

The account winds through the halls of political disturbance, where pioneers wrestle with the intricacies of administration and the heaviness of their choices. The beginning of Iron Will in the domain of governmental issues is exemplified by pioneers who transcend the conflict, directed by a feeling of obligation and a steadfast obligation to the government assistance of their constituents. Political upsets become cauldrons, testing the determination of the individuals who champion the reason for equity and correspondence.

In the chronicles of war, the adventure of Iron Will takes on a dismal tint, as troopers walk into the pot of contention with an emotionless assurance. The front line turns into a proving ground, where the determination of people and countries is estimated in the pot of battle. It is notwithstanding misfortune that the genuine strength of Iron Will arises, as troopers, limited by a typical reason, stand up to the cruel real factors of battle with boldness and flexibility.

The story goes to the domain of training, where understudies explore the maze of learning with a hunger for information and an assurance to conquer scholastic difficulties. The beginning of Iron Will in training is set apart by the extraordinary excursion of people who, despite everything, seek after scholarly greatness. An excursion rises above the bounds of homerooms, as understudies wrestle with the intricacies of their picked fields, driven by an energy to have a significant effect on the world.

As the story unfurls, we witness the convergence of innovation and human creativity, where the computerized age turns into a cauldron for development. The beginning of Iron Will in the mechanical area is portrayed by the steady quest for progress, as architects and trailblazers push the limits of what is conceivable. The computerized boondocks turns into a jungle gym for the individuals who really hope for a future molded by the combination of human inventiveness and innovative progression.

Think about the tale of a tech business person, exploring the consistently developing scene of the computerized world. Notwithstanding quick change and wild contest, the business visionary depends on the supply of Iron Will to adjust, develop, and remain on the ball.

It is in the cauldron of the tech business that the genuine soul of Iron Will is uncovered, as visionaries disturb laid out standards and prepare for another period of conceivable outcomes.

The account unfurls further into the field of civil rights, where activists and backers champion the reason for fairness and common freedoms. The beginning of Iron Will in the domain of civil rights is set apart by the unfaltering obligation to destroying foundational imbalances and cultivating a more comprehensive society. Activists, filled by an energy for equity, face the dug in designs of mistreatment with a boldness that rouses change.

Think about the narrative of a common freedoms lobbyist, testing severe systems and upholding for the voiceless. Despite abuse and risk, the lobbyist draws upon the wellspring of Iron Will to endure chasing after equity. It is in the pot of activism that the genuine force of Iron Will is released, as people and developments oppose the chances to achieve groundbreaking change.

The story grows to the domain of natural preservation, where stewards of the Earth face the critical difficulties of environmental change. The beginning of Iron Will in natural backing is portrayed by the assurance to shield the planet for people in the future. Progressives, researchers, and activists join in a typical reason, confronting the stupendous undertaking of switching ecological debasement with an unfaltering obligation to manageability.

Consider the narrative of a naturalist, working enthusiastically to safeguard imperiled species and save delicate environments. Notwithstanding lack of concern and natural emergencies, the tree hugger depends on the characteristic force of Iron Will to endure in the fight for the planet. It is in the cauldron of ecological activism that the unyielding soul of Iron Will merges with the basic of saving the sensitive equilibrium of nature.

The account goes to the domain of medical services, where clinical experts face the heap difficulties of mending and easing languishing. The beginning of Iron Will in medical services is exemplified by the eager endeavors of specialists, medical caretakers, and medical services laborers who explore the intricacies of the clinical field with a commitment to saving lives. In the pot of the medical care framework, these people defy the delicacy of human life with a versatility that rises above the limits of physical and profound depletion.

Consider the narrative of a specialist amidst a worldwide pandemic, working indefatigably to treat patients and relieve the effect of a destructive infection. Notwithstanding overpowering misfortune and the tireless requests of the medical services emergency, the specialist depends on the supply of Iron Will to proceed with the battle against an undetectable adversary. It is in the pot of medical services that the genuine bravery of Iron Will is uncovered, as clinical experts stand on the forefronts, defying the cruel real factors of sickness with relentless assurance.

The story closes by getting back to the overall subject of the beginning of Iron Will — a power that pervades each feature of human experience. From the singular battles of specialists and guardians to the aggregate undertakings of countries and developments, the narrative of Iron Will is a demonstration of the persevering through limit of the human soul to win over misfortune.

In the stupendous embroidery of presence, the beginning of Iron Will is a consistently unfurling account — a story that rises above the limits of existence. A power shapes predeterminations, produces heritages, and pushes mankind forward on the excursion of progress. As we explore the mind boggling strings of this story, we come to understand that the beginning of Iron Will is definitely not a solitary occasion however a nonstop cycle — a never-ending fashioning of the human soul in the cauldron of life's difficulties.

1.1 Introduction to the concept of developing mental resilience and determination

In the complex dance of life, where difficulties proliferate and vulnerabilities loom, the human brain arises as an impressive hero — a supply of likely ready to be opened. At the center of this intellectual capacity lies the idea of creating mental strength and assurance — a powerful interaction of mental determination, versatile strategies for dealing with hardship or stress, and an enduring will to explore the intricacies of presence.

Mental flexibility, frequently compared to a mental defensive layer, is the capacity to return quickly from difficulty, to endure the tempests of existence without capitulating to the heavy deluge of difficulties. It is a necessary part of mental prosperity, engaging people to stand up to difficulties, defeat snags, and arise more grounded even with affliction. The beginning of mental strength can be followed to the multifaceted trap of mental, close to home, and conduct factors that shape a singular's reaction to life's preliminaries.

One of the foundations of mental flexibility is the development of a development outlook — a worldview that sees difficulties as any open doors for development as opposed to unfavorable boundaries. Embracing a development mentality includes encouraging a conviction that capacities and insight can be created through devotion and difficult work. This attitude shift reevaluates mishaps as venturing stones to advance, empowering people to see disappointments not as decisive endpoints but rather as important examples in the excursion of personal development.

Past the mental domains, the capacity to understand individuals on a deeper level arises as a crucial part of mental strength. The capacity to comprehend and manage one's feelings, as well as understand the feelings of others, outfits people with the profound readiness expected to explore the recurring pattern of life. Close to home strength includes recognizing and handling feelings in a productive way, considering a decent and versatile reaction to life's difficulties.

Additionally, the idea of mental versatility is entwined with the improvement of successful survival techniques. Versatile survival techniques engage people to oversee pressure, uneasiness, and misfortune in a way that advances mental prosperity. These methodologies might incorporate critical thinking, looking for social help, rethinking negative contemplations, and participating in exercises that encourage unwinding and revival. By developing a different tool stash of survival techniques, people upgrade their capacity to explore the horde challenges that life presents.

As mental flexibility frames the bedrock of mental strength, assurance arises as its dynamic partner — a main impetus that pushes people towards their objectives with steady concentration and determination. Assurance envelops a relentless obligation to accomplishing goals, even notwithstanding deterrents and difficulties. The fuel lights the fire of desire, changing yearnings into substantial real factors through constant exertion and versatility.

The beginning of assurance can be followed to inherent inspiration — the interior drive that propels people to seek after objectives for the sheer delight of authority and individual satisfaction. Characteristic inspiration stands out from extraneous inspiration, which is driven by outside remunerations or evasion of discipline. Developing assurance includes taking advantage of the wellspring of natural inspiration, adjusting individual qualities to objectives, and getting fulfillment from the excursion as much as the objective.

Moreover, the idea of assurance is intently attached to the improvement of coarseness — a quality portrayed by energy and steadiness over the long haul. Coarse people show a fearless obligation to their objectives, showing strength even with difficulties and a getting through energy for their interests. The development of coarseness includes embracing difficulties as any open doors for development, keeping a feeling of direction, and supporting exertion in spite of hindrances.

The transaction between mental versatility and assurance turns out to be especially striking chasing after long haul objectives. Whether making progress toward self-improvement, proficient achievement, or the acknowledgment of inventive undertakings, people experience a progression of preliminaries that test their purpose. The cooperative connection between mental versatility and assurance enables people to climate the unavoidable tempests, gain from disappointments, and continue chasing their goals.

In the domain of self-awareness, the excursion towards self-revelation and personal development is set apart by the requirement for mental strength and assurance. People setting out on the way of self-awareness frequently face inner obstructions — self-question, feeling of dread toward disappointment, and the uneasiness of venturing outside safe places. Mental versatility turns into the anchor that steadies people during snapshots of self-reflection and contemplation, permitting them to stand up to inward evil presences and arise with a more profound comprehension of themselves.

All the while, assurance fills the quest for individual objectives, whether they include procuring new abilities, developing solid propensities, or cultivating significant connections. The course of self-awareness requests supported exertion and an eagerness to stand up to the difficulties that emerge en route. Assurance turns into the main impetus that drives people through the pinnacles and valleys of self-revelation, guaranteeing they stay consistent with their desires.

In the expert field, the convergence of mental flexibility and assurance becomes obvious chasing profession objectives and goals. The cutting edge work environment is loaded with difficulties — furious rivalry, quick mechanical progressions, and the requests of a high speed, steadily developing scene. Exploring this expert landscape expects people to develop mental versatility, adjusting to change, and returning from difficulties with a strong soul.

Assurance, with regards to proficient achievement, includes defining aggressive objectives, fostering a smart course of action, and driving forward despite deterrents. The power enables people to transcend difficulties, gain from disappointments, and consistently refine their abilities and capabilities. The collaboration between mental versatility and assurance positions people to make due as well as flourish in the unique domain of expert pursuits.

Innovativeness and advancement, as well, are spaces where the idea of mental strength and assurance tracks down articulation. The innovative approach is innately full of vulnerability, vagueness, and the certainty of experiencing inventive blocks.

Mental flexibility turns into the impetus that empowers people to explore the turbulent waters of imagination, embracing the iterative idea of the inventive excursion.

Assurance, then again, pushes people to continue in the innovative approach in spite of impediments and self-question. The power forces specialists, authors, and pioneers to push the limits of their creative mind, explore different avenues regarding clever thoughts, and carry their inventive dreams to completion. The beginning of weighty advancements and creative show-stoppers frequently lies in the resolute assurance to change dynamic ideas into unmistakable real factors.

In the social and relational circle, the advancement of mental versatility and assurance is vital for building and supporting significant connections. Relational elements are loaded with difficulties — clashes, misconceptions, and the intricacies of exploring different characters. Mental flexibility furnishes people with the ability to understand individuals on a profound level and versatility expected to explore the complexities of human associations.

Assurance, with regards to connections, includes the obligation to supporting and supporting associations notwithstanding the inescapable difficulties. The power enables people to convey actually, resolve clashes helpfully, and contribute the time and exertion expected for significant associations. The cooperative connection between mental versatility and assurance cultivates strong people equipped for encouraging sound associations with sympathy and validness.

Instruction, as an extraordinary excursion of securing information and abilities, is one more field where the idea of mental strength and assurance is of fundamental significance. Understudies, exploring the scholarly scene, experience a bunch of difficulties — scholastic tensions, the anxiety toward disappointment, and the need to adjust different obligations. Mental versatility turns into the bedrock that enables understudies to adapt to scholarly pressure, oversee time actually, and quickly return from difficulties.

Assurance, with regards to instruction, includes the obligation to scholarly objectives, the steadiness expected for thorough review, and the flexibility to confront scholastic misfortunes with a development mentality. The union of mental strength and assurance positions understudies to succeed scholastically as well as foster an adoration for discovering that stretches out past the bounds of formal schooling.

In the more extensive cultural setting, the improvement of mental strength and assurance turns into an aggregate undertaking — a fundamental part for encouraging networks that can endure the hardships of progress and misfortune. Cultural difficulties, whether financial slumps, worldwide emergencies, or social treacheries, request an aggregate supply of mental flexibility to explore vulnerabilities and decide the course of aggregate activity.

Assurance, on a cultural scale, includes the obligation to shared values, the tirelessness expected for establishing fundamental change, and the flexibility to stand up to instilled social issues. The power drives networks to meet up despite difficulty, advocate for equity, and work towards making a more evenhanded and strong society. The beneficial interaction of mental flexibility and assurance turns into the main thrust behind cultural advancement and positive change.

In the computerized age, where the speed of progress is sped up, and people are assaulted with data and boosts, the development of mental flexibility and assurance takes on added importance. The consistent network and the requests of a speedy way of life present difficulties to mental prosperity, requiring a proactive way to deal with creating versatility despite computerized stressors.

Assurance, in the computerized setting, includes the purposeful utilization of innovation to line up with individual and expert objectives, the discipline to define limits for screen time, and the versatility to explore the advanced scene with a careful methodology. The amalgamation of mental versatility and assurance prepares people to tackle the advantages of innovation while relieving its possible pessimistic effect on psychological well-being.

As we set out on this investigation of the idea of creating mental flexibility and assurance, it is fundamental to perceive that these characteristics are not fixed qualities but rather powerful limits that can be developed and reinforced after some time.

The excursion towards mental versatility and assurance includes a promise to mindfulness, an eagerness to embrace difficulties as any open doors for development, and a commitment to nonstop learning and variation.

This investigation will dive into the complex features of mental flexibility and assurance, investigating commonsense systems, mental structures, and genuine models that enlighten the way towards developing these fundamental characteristics. From the complexities of exploring pressure and difficulty to the significant effect of flexibility and assurance on individual and aggregate prosperity, this investigation intends to give an extensive comprehension of the powerful interchange between the brain and the development of a versatile and decided soul.

In the parts that follow, we will disentangle the layers of mental versatility and assurance, looking at the mental rules that support these ideas and digging into commonsense methodologies for their turn of events. Through a union of examination discoveries, master experiences, and engaging stories, this investigation looks to engage people with the information and instruments expected to brace their psychological flexibility, develop assurance, and set out on an extraordinary excursion towards a stronger and decided life.

1.2 Personal stories of individuals who overcame obstacles through sheer willpower

The embroidered artwork of human experience is woven with strings of versatility, and inside its complicated examples lie accounts of people who, despite everything, called an exceptional supply of resolve to conquer apparently outlandish snags. These individual stories act as demonstrations of the dauntless soul that dwells inside every one of us — a soul equipped for prevailing over misfortune, opposing the limitations of situation, and outlining a course towards win. Here, we dig into the accounts of astounding people whose accounts enlighten the groundbreaking force of sheer resolution.

Consider the story of Sarah, a young lady naturally introduced to testing conditions in an underestimated local area. Brought up in a climate set apart by restricted assets and social burdens, Sarah confronted a horde of obstructions that might have directed her way of living. Notwithstanding, powered by an enduring assurance to break the pattern of generational affliction, Sarah submerged herself in schooling.

Against the background of financial difficulties, Sarah's obligation to her examinations turned into an encouraging sign. She explored a requesting scholastic excursion, frequently forfeiting relaxation and solace to seek after her fantasies. Her persistent self control drove her to succeed scholastically, tying down grants that gave a passage to advanced education. Through sheer assurance, Sarah not just opposed the impediments forced by her conditions yet in addition turned into a motivation to others locally, demonstrating that the force of will can rise above even the most dug in hindrances.

Essentially, the narrative of James, a carefully prepared business visionary, mirrors the constancy of the human soul when confronted with difficulties in the business world. James set out on his innovative excursion with a dream to reform an industry however experienced unanticipated difficulties that took steps to wreck his desires. Despite monetary emergencies, market changes, and doubtful partners, James showed steady resolution.

Instead of surrendering to the heaviness of misfortune, James turned, adjusting his methodologies and refining his plan of action. The innovative scene is loaded with vulnerabilities, yet James' flexibility and assurance turned into the main impetus behind his capacity to weather conditions storms that would have put numerous others down. His story highlights the extraordinary capability of sheer self discipline in exploring the complicated landscape of business and arising unblemished as well as more grounded and stronger.

The domain of actual difficulties likewise gives a material to accounts of exceptional resolution. Take, for example, the story of Emma, a competitor whose life went off in a strange direction while a crippling mishap left her deadened starting from the waist. Confronted with the possibility of a radically changed life, Emma faced a decision — capitulate to surrender or bring the internal solidarity to rethink her capacities.

Emma picked the last option.

Through extreme restoration and an unshakeable will to recover organization over her life, Emma left on an excursion of physical and mental change. Her story is one of steadiness, as she adjusted to her new reality as well as embraced sports for of demonstrating that actual impediments could be risen above through sheer self discipline. Emma's strength on the athletic field turned into a signal of motivation, showing the way that the human soul, energized by resolute assurance, could win over the most imposing actual difficulties.

In the field of wellbeing and health, the narrative of Imprint fills in as a piercing representation of the extraordinary force of resolution even with perilous disease.

Determined to have an intriguing and forceful type of disease, Imprint stood up to a guess that generally ruled out good faith. Nonetheless, as opposed to capitulating to surrender, Imprint decided to marshal each ounce of his psychological strength and self discipline to go up against the ailment head-on.

Imprint's process included thorough clinical medicines as well as a significant obligation to mental and close to home prosperity. Through reflection, perception, and an unflinching faith in his capacity to defeat the chances, Imprint made due as well as flourished. His story turned into a demonstration of the harmonious connection between mental strength and actual recuperating — a demonstration of the exceptional accomplishments that can be accomplished when self control turns into a directing power even with life's gravest difficulties.

In the domain of imaginative pursuits, the story of Maya, a yearning craftsman, reveals insight into the extraordinary capability of self control chasing energy. Maya's process was loaded with cultural assumptions and monetary limitations that might have smothered her imaginative desires. However, furnished with a faithful assurance to communicate her thoughts through workmanship, Maya explored the impediments that took steps to darken her innovative way.

Maya's story is one of penance and responsibility. Confronted with the need to shuffle numerous tasks to help her creative undertakings, she displayed a persistent hard working attitude that rose above the domains of depletion. Her self control turned into the main thrust behind her capacity to sharpen her specialty, make reminiscent masterpieces, and ultimately gather acknowledgment for her gifts. Maya's process remains as a demonstration of the extraordinary force of self control chasing innovative satisfaction, demonstrating that enthusiasm, when powered by relentless assurance, can conquer even the most considerable difficulties.

The story of Alex, an overcomer of habit, epitomizes the extraordinary excursion that unfurls when resolution turns into the impetus for beating individual devils. Confronted with the desolates of substance misuse, Alex defied a junction — a decision between surrendering to the damaging charm of habit or bringing the solidarity to break free. In the pot of restoration, Alex's resolve arose as an imposing partner in the fight for moderation.

Recuperation from dependence is an overly complex excursion set apart by backslides and snapshots of sadness. Alex's story, notwithstanding, is one of versatility and assurance, as every difficulty turned into a venturing stone toward enduring recuperation. The force of will appeared in Alex's capacity to revamp a daily existence that had been broken by habit, reviving connections, and tracking down reason chasing supported prosperity. His story reverberates as an epitome of the groundbreaking power innate in the human soul when filled by immovable assurance.

The story of Maria, an overcomer of aggressive behavior at home, enlightens the groundbreaking force of resolution with regards to recovering organization and reconstructing life after injury. Maria persevered through a frightening trial that might have sustained patterns of exploitation, yet her story took an alternate direction. Energized by an unflinching will to break liberated from the shackles of misuse, Maria looked for shelter and backing, exploring the intricacies of legitimate and inner difficulties.

Maria's story embodies the strength that arises when resolution turns into an impetus for freedom. Her process included actual getaway as well as a significant mental change. With assurance as her compass, Maria endure the injury as well as arisen as a backer for other people, directing her encounters into a power for social change. Her story highlights the limit of self control to break the chains of exploitation and make ready for strong, engaged survivors.

With regards to schooling, the story of Raj, an understudy from an impeded foundation, grandstands the groundbreaking capability of determination chasing information and self-improvement. Raj stood up to foundational boundaries that might have smothered his instructive yearnings, yet his story turned into a demonstration of the flexibility that arises when self discipline turns into the main thrust for scholarly accomplishment.

Confronted with restricted assets and cultural assumptions that misrepresented his true capacity, Raj displayed a voracious long for learning. Through extended periods of time of self-study, determination even with scholastic difficulties, and a relentless obligation to his instructive objectives, Raj rose above the limits forced by his conditions. His process fills in as a signal of motivation, exhibiting that self discipline, when tackled chasing information, can hoist people past the requirements of cultural assumptions.

These individual stories meet to shape a mosaic of human encounters, each recounting a novel story of win over difficulty through sheer resolution. Whether in the domains of schooling, business venture, actual difficulties, wellbeing, imagination, compulsion recuperation, or defeating injury, the consistent idea is the groundbreaking power that arises when people gather the profundities of their inward strength.

These accounts rise above the domains of individual accomplishments, reverberating as general declarations to the vast limit of the human soul to go up against, persevere, and rise above. Every story highlights the harmonious connection between mental versatility and sheer assurance — a partnership that changes difficulties into potential open doors, misfortunes into venturing stones, and affliction into the cauldron for individual and aggregate development.

As we consider these individual stories, we are reminded that inside each individual lives an undiscovered repository of determination — a power ready to be outfit, developed, and coordinated towards extraordinary finishes. These accounts move not just by exhibiting the victories of the human soul yet additionally by filling in as guides that enlighten the way for others confronting their own afflictions.

Basically, the individual accounts of these people weave a story that commends the unprecedented likely intrinsic in the human experience — a possible that, when strengthened by determination, turns into an impetus for flexibility.

1.3 Establishing the connection between mental strength and physical transformation

The unpredictable exchange between mental strength and actual change shapes the foundation of an all encompassing way to deal with prosperity. The brain body association, frequently thought to be a mystical idea, tracks down observational approval in the harmonious connection between mental grit and actual wellbeing. This association isn't just narrative; logical examination uncovers the significant effect that psychological strength can apply on the body, affecting everything from actual execution to the resistant framework and recuperation from ailment. This investigation digs into the complex elements of the psychological actual association, disentangling the components that highlight the extraordinary force of a versatile brain in molding a vigorous, solid body.

Actual change is a wide and enveloping term, going from athletic ability and solid improvement to in general wellbeing and life span. Numerous people set out on wellness ventures with explicit objectives, whether it be weight reduction, muscle gain, worked on cardiovascular wellbeing, or upgraded athletic execution. While exercise and sustenance without a doubt assume vital parts in accomplishing these goals, the psychological part — frequently consigned to the outskirts — is arising as a basic determinant of progress.

Think about the situation of a singular endeavoring to shed pounds and take on a better way of life. The excursion ordinarily includes addresses in dietary propensities and the fuse of ordinary activity. In any case, the psychological strength to stick to these changes, particularly even with difficulties and mishaps, is many times the key part that decides the direction of progress.

Research demonstrates that the attitude with which people approach their wellness objectives altogether impacts results. A review distributed in the Diary of Heftiness showed that people who developed an uplifting perspective toward practice and saw it as a wellspring of euphoria were bound to stick to their wellness regimens. This positive outlook, described by inherent inspiration and an emphasis on the delight in active work, cultivated long haul adherence and added to supported actual change.

The psychological solidarity to beat obstructions is especially clear in the domain of actual preparation. Competitors, whether experts or novices, frequently experience levels, wounds, and the repetitiveness of preparing schedules. At these times, mental flexibility turns into the main thrust that moves people to continue on. A concentrate in the Diary of Applied Game Brain research featured the relationship between's mental flexibility and athletic execution, proposing that competitors with more elevated levels of strength were better prepared to explore difficulties and keep up with max operation.

Moreover, the effect of weight on actual wellbeing couldn't possibly be more significant. Persistent pressure sets off a fountain of physiological reactions, including the arrival of cortisol — a chemical related with the body's instinctive reaction. Raised cortisol levels overstretched periods add to a scope of medical problems, from weight gain to hindered insusceptible capability. Mental strength, appeared through pressure the board methods, for example, care and unwinding works out, can moderate the unfriendly impacts of persistent pressure, encouraging a more helpful climate for actual prosperity.

The multifaceted dance between mental strength and actual change is additionally obvious in the area of strong turn of events. Past the mechanical parts of lifting loads and participating in opposition preparing, the brain assumes a critical part in accomplishing ideal outcomes.

Consider the peculiarity of muscle hypertrophy, the cycle by which muscle filaments expansion in size. While nourishment and exercise are principal, the psychological part of preparing — concentration, expectation, and the brain muscle association — can intensify the adequacy of opposition preparing.

Research in the field of sports brain science underscores the meaning of the psyche muscle association, wherein people purposely concentrate on the muscles being worked during obstruction works out. This deliberate center improves the enrollment of muscle strands and adds to more noteworthy muscle commitment. Mental strength, as appeared through focus and a brain receptive to the complexities of development, in this manner turns into an instrumental consider chiseling and upgrading strong turn of events.

Besides, the psychological solidarity to persevere through actual inconvenience is a sign of the people who go through thorough preparation. Whether participating in extreme cardio exercise, high-intensity games, or strength preparing, the capacity to push through distress is a psychological property that recognizes the people who accomplish extraordinary actual outcomes. This psychological strength is in many cases created through moderate openness to testing circumstances, continuously extending the singular's edge for distress and making ready for more prominent actual variations.

The connection between mental strength and actual change stretches out to the domain of cardiovascular wellbeing. Ordinary high-impact practice is a foundation of cardiovascular wellness, adding to heart wellbeing and generally speaking prosperity. In any case, the psychological parts of activity adherence and the mental reaction to cardiovascular preparation are significant supporters of its adequacy.

People with more significant levels of mental flexibility are bound to stick to cardiovascular activity regimens. This adherence is critical for receiving the drawn out rewards of worked on cardiovascular wellbeing. The American Heart Affiliation highlights the significance of standard vigorous practice in decreasing the gamble of coronary illness and suggests somewhere around 150 minutes of moderate-force practice each week. The psychological solidarity to support this degree of active work, in spite of the contending requests of day to day existence, highlights the unique exchange between mental grit and cardiovascular prosperity.

Besides, the psychological solidarity to push through apparent effort during cardiovascular activity is a vital calculate improving its advantages. The Rating of Seen Effort (RPE) is an emotional proportion of how hard a singular feels they are working during exercise. Studies have demonstrated the way that people who can endure more significant levels of seen effort during high-impact practice frequently accomplish predominant cardiovascular wellness results. This psychological versatility to persevere and persist, in any event, when confronted with the physiological uneasiness of supported exertion, adds to the extraordinary effect of cardiovascular preparation.

The insusceptible framework, a complicated organization of cells and proteins intended to safeguard the body against contamination and illness, is one more physiological space impacted by mental strength. Ongoing pressure, frequently connected to negative mental states, has been displayed to smother the resistant reaction, delivering people more helpless to ailments. Then again, positive mental states, like idealism and versatility, have been related with improved resistant capability.

Research in psychoneuroimmunology — the investigation of the cooperation between mental cycles and the resistant framework — demonstrates that pressure decrease procedures, like care contemplation, can decidedly affect safe capability. The brain's capacity to adjust the safe reaction highlights the basic job mental strength plays in reinforcing the body's guards and adding to generally speaking wellbeing.

The helpful force of rest, a major part of actual prosperity, is likewise complicatedly connected to mental states. Mental strength, especially the capacity to oversee pressure and manage feelings, assumes a crucial part in advancing sound rest designs. People with elevated degrees of stress or mental turmoil frequently experience rest unsettling influences, which, after some time, can injuriously affect actual wellbeing.

The bidirectional connection between psychological well-being and rest is clear in examinations showing that unfortunate rest adds to uplifted feelings of anxiety and profound reactivity. The psychological strength to execute rest cleanliness rehearses, lay out a steady rest schedule, and oversee pressure before sleep time adds to helpful rest — a fundamental part of actual recuperation and change.

Moreover, the psychological solidarity to explore life changes and adjust to changing conditions is a critical determinant of long haul actual prosperity. Life altering situations, whether positive or negative, can affect wellbeing ways of behaving and schedules. People with more elevated levels of mental strength are better prepared to conform to life changes, keep up with solid propensities, and explore the intricacies of current living without undermining their actual wellbeing.

The connection between mental strength and actual change stretches out to the mind boggling organizations of chemicals that control different physiological cycles. Cortisol, frequently named the "stress chemical," is delivered because of stress and assumes a part in digestion, resistant capability, and fiery reactions. Persistent pressure, energized by bad mental states, can dysregulate cortisol levels, adding to metabolic irregular characteristics and aggravation.

On the other hand, mental versatility and positive profound states have been related with more versatile cortisol reactions. Studies propose that people with more significant levels of mental strength display a better cortisol profile, with lower levels of cortisol in light of stressors.

This cortisol guideline is ensnared in metabolic wellbeing, weight the board, and in general actual prosperity.

The effect of mental strength on actual change additionally stretches out to the endocrine framework, including chemicals, for example, adrenaline and noradrenaline, which assume vital parts in the body's pressure reaction and energy activation. The psychological strength to stand up to difficulties, combined with the capacity to oversee pressure successfully, adds to a fair pressure reaction that works with actual versatility and ideal energy usage.

The groundbreaking force of mental strength turns out to be especially articulated with regards to ongoing circumstances and the recuperation from ailment. People confronting wellbeing challenges, whether ongoing infections or intense sicknesses, frequently explore physical and profound intricacies that require a tough outlook. Concentrates on in psychosomatic medication feature the bidirectional connection between mental states and wellbeing results, showing the way that psychological strength can emphatically impact the course of sickness and recuperation.

The psyche's impact on torment discernment is a convincing part of this relationship. Ongoing torment conditions, frequently described by a perplexing transaction of physical and mental variables, feature the job of mental versatility in overseeing and moderating torment. Mind-body mediations, for example, mental conduct treatment and care based approaches, have been displayed to influence torment insight and utilitarian results decidedly.

Moreover, the psychological solidarity to develop an inspirational perspective and keep a feeling of direction during disease has been related with further developed wellbeing results. Research in psychoneuroimmunology recommends that people with a hopeful attitude show upgraded resistant reactions, working with recuperation from sicknesses going from irresistible illnesses to constant circumstances.

The psychological solidarity to stick to clinical medicines, take part in rehabilitative endeavors, and embrace wellbeing advancing ways of behaving is a basic part of actual recuperation. Whether beating the difficulties of recovery after medical procedure or exploring the intricacies of dealing with a constant condition, people with elevated degrees of mental flexibility frequently display more prominent adherence to therapy regimens, adding to better wellbeing results.

With regards to persistent infections like diabetes, cardiovascular circumstances, or immune system problems, the psychological solidarity to embrace way of life adjustments and deal with the close to home cost of sickness becomes fundamental. Studies show that psychosocial mediations, including care based pressure decrease and mental conduct treatment, can decidedly affect results in people with constant sicknesses. The psychological mettle to face the multi-layered difficulties of ongoing circumstances highlights the extraordinary capability of a versatile brain in molding actual prosperity.

The job of mental strength in molding actual change isn't restricted to individual pursuits however stretches out to the more extensive setting of cultural prosperity. General wellbeing challenges, like stationary ways of life, unfortunate dietary propensities, and increasing paces of ongoing illnesses, highlight the requirement for aggregate endeavors to advance actual prosperity. Mental versatility at the cultural level includes cultivating conditions that help positive mental states, diminish stressors, and advance wellbeing improving ways of behaving.

In the domain of preventive medication, the psychological solidarity to embrace and support sound way of life propensities is basic. General wellbeing drives pointed toward advancing actual work, empowering nutritious eating, and addressing emotional well-being add to the prosperity of networks. The social determinants of wellbeing, which include monetary, natural, and psychosocial factors, highlight the interconnectedness of mental strength and actual prosperity on a cultural scale.

Instructive establishments assume a crucial part in forming the psychological and actual prosperity of people in the future. The development of mental flexibility, the capacity to appreciate individuals on a profound level, and stress the executives abilities inside instructive educational programs adds to the general soundness of understudies. Actual schooling programs that focus on active work as well as the improvement of a positive outlook toward wellness cultivate propensities that can enduringly affect deep rooted wellbeing.

Working environment conditions, where people spend a critical part of their waking hours, offer a ripe ground for advancing mental strength and actual prosperity. Corporate wellbeing programs that integrate systems for stress decrease, emotional well-being support, and active work add to a better labor force. The financial ramifications of an intellectually strong and truly sound labor force, described by decreased non-attendance and expanded efficiency, highlight the sweeping effect of this interconnected relationship.

Metropolitan preparation and configuration likewise assume a part in molding the psychological actual association. Admittance to green spaces, walkable networks, and sporting offices adds to a climate that upholds active work and mental prosperity. The idea of a "sound city" envelops the arrangement of medical care administrations as well as the making of conditions that cultivate mental flexibility and actual wellbeing.

As we explore this investigation of the association between mental strength and actual change, it becomes apparent that the division among brain and body is a fake develop. The psyche and body work as a coordinated framework, each impacting and forming the other in a unique dance of proportional causation. The extraordinary force of mental strength on actual prosperity features the requirement for an extensive way to deal with wellbeing — one that perceives the indivisible idea of mental and actual states.

All in all, the foundation of a strong association between mental strength and actual change isn't just observationally validated yet additionally resounds with the lived encounters of people endeavoring to upgrade their prosperity. Whether leaving on wellness ventures, exploring the intricacies of persistent circumstances, or adding to cultural drives for wellbeing advancement, the job of mental strength turns into an essential determinant of progress.

The extraordinary capability of mental strength incorporates domains as different as exercise adherence, solid turn of events, cardiovascular wellbeing, resistant capability, rest quality, and recuperation from ailment. From the microcosm of cell reactions to the world of cultural prosperity, the impact of mental flexibility on actual change saturates each feature of human life.

As we keep on disentangling the complexities of this powerful relationship, it is basic to perceive the singular organization that every individual has in developing mental strength and forming actual prosperity. The development of mental strength includes purposeful practices, like care, mental conduct methods, and stress the board, that engage people to explore the difficulties of existence with mettle.

The groundbreaking excursion toward improved mental strength and actual prosperity is certainly not a one-size-fits-all undertaking. It requires a nuanced comprehension of individual contrasts, inclinations, and necessities. Perceiving the interconnected idea of mental and actual states makes ready for customized ways to deal with wellbeing advancement — approaches that enable people to leave on groundbreaking excursions portrayed by flexibility, essentialness, and all encompassing prosperity.

Chapter 2

Forging the Mind: The Mental Blueprint

The human psyche, a multifaceted trap of contemplations, feelings, and insights, fills in as the focal point of our reality. It is the material whereupon the rich embroidered artwork of our encounters, recollections, and desires is woven. To comprehend the intricacies of the brain is to set out on an excursion through the maze of comprehension, investigating the actual embodiment of what makes us remarkably human.

At its center, the brain is a powerful substance, continually adjusting and developing in light of the outer and inner improvements that shape our lives. It's anything but a static diagram yet a moldable construction, equipped for fashioning new pathways and associations as time passes. The psychological plan, subsequently, is definitely not an unbending plan scratched in stone yet a liquid guide that outlines the course of our scholarly and close to home scenes.

The underpinning of the psychological outline lies in the perplexing organization of neurons that structure the premise of the cerebrum. These brain associations, similar to the strings of an embroidery, wind around together to make the examples of our viewpoints and activities. The most common way of fashioning the psyche starts in the beginning phases of improvement, as an infant's mind goes through a noteworthy excursion of development and refinement.

As babies, we are brought into the world with an immense potential for learning and transformation. The brain circuits that oversee essential capabilities like sight, hearing, and contact are as of now present, yet it is through experience that these circuits are tweaked and reinforced. The early long stretches of life become a basic period for producing the fundamental components of the psychological outline.

The climate assumes a crucial part in significantly shaping the psyche during this developmental stage. Cooperations with parental figures, openness to upgrades, and the nature of early encounters add to the foundation of brain processes that will impact mental and close to home turn of events. Positive communications, enhanced conditions, and supporting connections lay the preparation for a versatile and even mental outline.

Alternately, unfavorable encounters, disregard, or injury can engrave enduring consequences for the creating mind. The scars of early misfortune might appear as mental difficulties, profound aggravations, or personal conduct standards that persevere into adulthood. Understanding the effect of early encounters on the psychological outline reveals insight into the multifaceted transaction among nature and sustain in molding the human mind.

As people progress through life, the manufacturing of the brain go on through a persistent course of learning and transformation. The mind's amazing pliancy considers the arrangement of new brain associations and the rebuilding of existing ones because of new encounters. This flexibility is clear in the manner people obtain new abilities, explore novel difficulties, and absorb data from the steadily impacting world around them.

Schooling, both formal and casual, turns into an integral asset in the possession of those trying to shape their psychological outline. The obtaining of information, the advancement of decisive reasoning abilities, and the development of scholarly interest add to the refinement of mental cycles. The homeroom, the research facility, and the more extensive scene of life itself act as fields for the continuous development of the psyche's engineering.

Past the domain of training, the social and social settings in which people end up assume a critical part in forming the psychological plan. Social qualities, cultural standards, and relational connections impact the manner in which people see themselves as well as other people. The shared perspective of a local area leaves a permanent engraving on the personalities of its individuals, adding to the variety of mental diagrams across various societies and social orders.

The manufacturing of the psyche stretches out past the mental space to include the unpredictable woven artwork of feelings. Feelings, frequently viewed as the range of the brain, add profundity and variety to the human experience. The exchange between mental cycles and profound reactions makes a nuanced scene that characterizes the extravagance of our inward lives.

The capacity to appreciate people on a profound level, the capacity to perceive, comprehend, and deal with one's feelings, turns into a vital component in the producing of a strong and genuinely adjusted mind. The development of compassion, mindfulness, and relational abilities adds to the advancement of people who can explore the intricacies of human associations with beauty and awareness.

Nonetheless, the producing of the psyche isn't without its difficulties. Emotional wellness, a basic part of generally speaking prosperity, mirrors the condition of the psyche's outline. The predominance of psychological well-being issues highlights the significance of tending to the intricacies and weaknesses intrinsic in the human mind.

Stress, injury, hereditary inclinations, and ecological elements can all add to the rise of psychological well-being difficulties. The shame encompassing psychological wellness issues frequently upsets people from looking for the help and assets they need. To produce a versatile and flourishing brain, it is fundamental for encourage a culture that focuses on psychological wellness, destigmatizes looking for help, and gives open assets to those out of luck.

The job of innovation in forming the psychological diagram can't be neglected. In the advanced age, the consistent flood of data, the pervasiveness of online entertainment, and the universality of screens present the two open doors and difficulties for mental prosperity. The computerized scene can be a wellspring of association, information, and inventiveness, however it likewise acts dangers such like data over-burden, social correlation, and the disintegration of certifiable human associations.

The effect of innovation on the creating mind, especially in the more youthful age, prompts reflection on the harmony among virtual and certifiable encounters. As people explore the computerized scene, it becomes basic to develop computerized proficiency, care, and sound limits to guarantee a positive impact on the psychological plan.

The producing of the psyche is a long lasting excursion, and the later phases of life bring their own arrangement of contemplations. As people age, the brain goes through normal changes in mental capability. While a few mental capacities might decline with age, others might keep on thriving. The idea of brain adaptability, the mind's capacity to adjust and revamp itself, stays significant all through the life expectancy, offering expect development and learned.

The quest for mental essentialness in later life includes participating in exercises that animate the psyche, keeping up with social associations, and taking on a sound way of life. Mental save, the mind's capacity to endure age-related changes, is worked through a long period of scholarly pursuits, social commitment, and generally speaking prosperity. The decisions made in midlife and past add to the versatility and flexibility of the maturing mind.

In the great embroidery of human experience, the producing of the psyche is a common excursion that rises above individual limits. The shared perspective of mankind mirrors the entirety of individual mental outlines, each contributing a remarkable string to the complicated texture of our common presence. The difficulties and wins, the delights and distresses, all find articulation in the kaleidoscope of brains that populate our reality.

The investigation of the psychological diagram reaches out past the limits of science and brain research to incorporate the domains of reasoning, otherworldliness, and artistic expression. Scholars since the beginning of time have considered the idea of the brain, diving into inquiries of cognizance, character, and the significance of presence. The convergence of science and reasoning opens a passage to a more profound comprehension of the secrets that cover the inward operations of the brain.

Otherworldly practices, as well, offer experiences into the idea of the psyche, frequently outlining it as a vessel for higher cognizance or heavenly association. Practices like reflection, examination, and care give devices to people to investigate the profundities of their own personalities and develop a feeling of inward harmony and congruity.

Human expression, with their ability to bring out feeling, incite thought, and rouse imagination, act as a mirror to the human condition. Writing, music, visual expressions, and different types of imaginative articulation offer a window into the personalities of craftsmen, welcoming crowds to interface with the widespread parts of the human experience. The crossing point of craftsmanship and brain science enlightens the manners by which innovative articulation can shape and be formed by the psychological outline.

Chasing understanding the psychological diagram, the idea of cognizance arises as a focal riddle. Cognizance, the emotional consciousness of one's viewpoints, sentiments, and encounters, stays an outskirts of investigation that resists simple clarification. Speculations proliferate, going from the possibility that cognizance arises exclusively from the intricacy of brain organizations to additional magical ideas of cognizance as a principal part of the universe.

The investigation of changed conditions of cognizance, whether initiated by reflection, hallucinogenics, or different means, offers a brief look into the liquid idea of human mindfulness. These states challenge traditional ideas of the brain and give rich ground to investigating the secrets of cognizance. The investigation of awareness stretches out past the bounds of logical request, welcoming thought on the idea of the real world and the substance of being alive.

As we ponder the producing of the brain and the complexities of the psychological outline, it becomes clear that the excursion is an unending unfurling, a constant course of becoming. The psyche, with its limitless limit with respect to development and change, challenges simple classification or decrease to a bunch of foreordained designs. It is a powerful element, a living demonstration of the steadily unfurling story of the human experience.

In the excellent embroidery of presence, the psychological outline is a magnum opus really taking shape, a continuous masterpiece that mirrors the aggregate yearnings, battles, and wins of humankind. To produce the psyche is to take part in a cognizant and purposeful investigation of the inward domains, an excursion that requires both self-reflection and a profound appreciation for the interconnectedness, everything being equal.

The manufacturing of the psyche is an obligation and an honor — an obligation to sustain our own psychological prosperity and an honor to contribute decidedly to the aggregate mental scene. It is a source of inspiration, encouraging people to develop mindfulness, embrace long lasting learning, and cultivate a culture that focuses on the prosperity of psyches across different networks and social orders.

As we explore the intricacies of the cutting edge world, the producing of the brain takes on restored importance. The difficulties of the computerized age, the tensions of a high speed society, and the worldwide interconnectivity of human encounters highlight the requirement for a careful and purposeful way to deal with mental prosperity.

It is a call for equilibrium, strength, and a profound feeling of interconnectedness that rises above individual, social, and cultural limits.

2.1 Exploring the psychology of discipline and focus

Discipline and concentration, two mainstays of mental ability, assume necessary parts in forming our way of living. In the complicated woven artwork of human brain science, these characteristics arise as key parts that overcome any issues among goals and accomplishments. As we leave on the excursion of understanding the subtleties of discipline and concentration, we unwind the complicated strings that wind through the texture of our mental cycles.

Discipline, frequently inseparable from poise and limitation, is a mental develop that includes the guideline of one's viewpoints, feelings, and ways of behaving. The power empowers people with comply to a bunch of rules, standards, or objectives notwithstanding the presence of interruptions, enticements, or hindrances. Discipline, in its quintessence, is the quiet modeler of character, establishing the groundwork for strength, determination, and self-improvement.

The underlying foundations of discipline dig into the domain of leader works, a bunch of mental cycles housed in the prefrontal cortex of the mind. These chief capabilities incorporate a scope of capacities, including working memory, mental adaptability, and inhibitory control. Working in show, these mental cycles structure the brain platform whereupon discipline is assembled.

The improvement of discipline starts in the cauldron of young life, as people figure out how to explore the landscape of rules, limits, and assumptions set via guardians and society. The early years become a preparation ground for the development of discretion, as youngsters wrestle with the motivations of moment delight and the thriving consciousness of cultural standards.

Parental direction, instructive conditions, and cultural designs contribute essentially to the development of discipline in people. The consistency of rules, the demonstrating of discretion by power figures, and the support of positive ways of behaving make the platform whereupon the structure of discipline is raised. As people navigate the scenes of immaturity and adulthood, the discipline imparted in their early stages turns into a directing power, impacting decisions, propensities, and long haul results.

Discipline, nonetheless, is definitely not a static quality; a powerful cycle requires ceaseless exertion and refinement. The interchange between natural inspiration and outside factors shapes the direction of restrained ways of behaving. Natural inspiration, coming from individual qualities, interests, or a feeling of direction, fills in as a strong fuel for supported discipline. Outside factors, like prizes, outcomes, and social endorsement, may go about as impetuses that reinforce or challenge the upkeep of discipline.

The brain research of discipline meets with the idea of determination, a limited at this point sustainable asset that oversees the capacity to apply restraint. The "strength" of one's resolve can be affected by elements like exhaustion, stress, and the mental burden forced by direction. Understanding the back and forth movement of determination gives bits of knowledge into the difficulties people face in keeping up with discipline, particularly despite contending requests and allurements.

The excursion of discipline interweaves with the quest for long haul objectives, whether scholarly, expert, or individual. Objective setting turns into a guide that channels discipline toward explicit goals, giving an internal compass and motivation. The brain research of objective pursuit uncovers the complicated dance between transient satisfaction and postponed rewards, as people explore the pressure between the craving for guaranteed delight and the obligation to future achievement.

In the domain of discipline, propensities arise as strong partners or imposing enemies. Propensities, instilled examples of conduct that become programmed after some time, can either build up focused activities or subvert them. The brain science of propensity arrangement digs into the brain systems that support propensity circles, from sign and routine to remunerate, and investigates the techniques for developing positive propensities that line up with trained living.

The convergence of discipline and center becomes obvious as we dig into the mental cycles that administer consideration and focus. Center, the capacity to coordinate consideration toward a particular errand or objective, is a mental expertise that underlies restrained activity. The human attentional framework, impacted by elements like excitement, oddity, and individual pertinence, shapes the elements of concentration in regular day to day existence.

Attentional control, a part of chief capabilities, assumes an essential part in keeping up with center in the midst of interruptions. The capacity to channel superfluous data, shift consideration when fundamental, and support center around a picked task adds to the fruitful execution of restrained activities. Attentional slips, whether because of outside upgrades or interior meandering considerations, present difficulties to supported center and require systems for alleviation.

The brain science of center stretches out to the idea of stream, a condition of ideal experience where people are completely drenched and retained in a difficult and remunerating movement. Accomplishing stream requires a sensitive harmony between expertise level and errand trouble, giving an ideal test that enraptures consideration and evokes a feeling of dominance. The development of stream encounters upgrades center and adds to the delight and satisfaction got from trained attempts.

Qualifications emerge among outside and inward factors that impact center. Outside factors envelop the actual climate, mechanical interruptions, and the requests of the outer world. Interior elements dive into the domains of mental cycles, profound states, and individual contrasts in attentional control. The exchange among outer and inward factors shapes the mental scene in which center works, impacting the simplicity or trouble of keeping up with consideration on a picked task.

The cutting edge time, set apart by the pervasiveness of computerized innovations, presents a remarkable arrangement of difficulties to concentration and discipline. The steady blast of notices, the appeal of web-based entertainment, and the enticement of moment satisfaction present dangers to supported consideration. The advanced scene, while offering phenomenal admittance to data and network, expects people to explore carefully to safeguard the respectability of their concentration and discipline.

The brain science of discipline and concentrate likewise meets with the idea of self-guideline, the capacity to screen and balance one's considerations, feelings, and ways of behaving. Self-guideline envelops the more extensive space of close to home guideline, drive control, and the regulation of stress reactions. The development of self-administrative abilities adds to the amicable coordination of discipline and concentration into day to day existence.

The job of care arises as a powerful partner in the development of discipline and concentration. Care, the act of non-critical familiarity with the current second, upgrades attentional control and profound guideline. The development of care abilities through reflection, breath mindfulness, or other scrutinizing rehearses gives people apparatuses to explore the intricacies of the psyche and support their ability for supported discipline and concentration.

As we explore the mental territory of discipline and concentration, the idea of inspiration surfaces as a main impetus that pushes people toward their objectives. Inspiration, the invigorating power that starts, supports, and coordinates conduct, includes a range of sources, from natural drives to outward rewards. The transaction among natural and outward inspiration shapes the quality and toughness of discipline chasing after objectives.

The self-assurance hypothesis, a structure in inspiration brain research, sets that people have natural mental requirements for independence, capability, and relatedness. Satisfying these requirements encourages natural inspiration, prompting a feeling of individual organization and volition in objective pursuit. Understanding the subtleties of inspiration gives bits of knowledge into the switches that can be pulled to support discipline and support center over an extended time.

The brain research of discipline and center broadens its venture into the domain of delaying, a typical test that torments objective coordinated ways of behaving. Stalling, the deferral of planned activities regardless of knowing the unfortunate results, mirrors the complex interaction between inspiration, self-guideline, and the evasion of aversive assignments. Unwinding the mental underpinnings of hesitation uncovers the systems for beating this universal enemy and invigorating discipline.

The cultural and social elements of discipline and center add layers of intricacy to the mental scene. Social standards, cultural assumptions, and the qualities implanted in friendly designs impact the arrangement and articulation of discipline. The idea of "aggregate foam," a term from social scientist Emile Durkheim, features the public experience of shared customs and exercises that encourage an aggregate concentration and discipline.

In the working environment, the brain research of discipline and center appears in the elements of efficiency, using time productively, and worker commitment. Bosses and pioneers assume urgent parts in establishing conditions that help restrained work propensities and supported center. The arrangement of hierarchical objectives with individual desires, the arrangement of assets, and the encouraging of a positive work culture add to the development of discipline and concentration among representatives.

The schooling system fills in as a cauldron for the improvement of discipline and concentration in the more youthful age. The construction of instructive conditions, the nature of educating, and the emotionally supportive networks set up all impact understudies' capacity to develop

restrained concentrate on propensities and supported center around scholarly errands. Methodologies for improving understudy inspiration, cultivating a development outlook, and showing leader capabilities become fundamental parts of successful training.

The brain research of discipline and center interweaves with the idea of coarseness, a quality described by energy and diligence toward long haul objectives. Coarseness, as proposed by clinician Angela Duckworth, mirrors the endurance and strength expected to climate misfortunes and continue even with difficulties. The development of coarseness includes a marriage of discipline and energy, making a synergistic power that pushes people toward the accomplishment of their most loved goals.

In the more extensive setting of emotional well-being, the brain research of discipline and center expects a urgent job in flexibility and prosperity. The capacity to control one's considerations and feelings, to support consideration on significant exercises, and to endure notwithstanding misfortune adds to mental and close to home thriving. Systems, for example, mental conduct mediations, care based approaches, and positive brain research intercessions offer roads for reinforcing discipline and concentration in the help of psychological wellness.

The entwining strings of discipline and center wind through the accounts of uncommon people who have made permanent imprints on history. The life stories of trailblazers, creators, specialists, and pioneers uncover the restrained propensities, centered endeavors, and strength that impelled them to significance. The narratives of these people act as guides of motivation, outlining the groundbreaking force of restrained living and centered try.

2.2 Techniques for developing a strong mindset for fitness goals

The quest for wellness isn't exclusively an actual undertaking; similarly a psychological excursion requests flexibility, discipline, and a hearty outlook. A solid mentality fills in as the bedrock whereupon effective wellness objectives are constructed, enabling people to conquer difficulties, remain committed, and accomplish enduring changes. In investigating the procedures for developing a strong mentality in the domain of wellness, we dig into the mental methodologies that support the quest for actual prosperity.

1. **Objective Setting and Lucidity:**
    The groundwork of a solid outlook in wellness starts with clear and reasonable objective setting. Laying out unambiguous, quantifiable, feasible, important,

and time-bound (Brilliant) objectives gives a guide to the wellness venture. Lucidity about the ideal results, whether it's weight reduction, muscle gain, or further developed perseverance, empowers people to actually channel their endeavors. Separating overall objectives into more modest, feasible achievements encourages a feeling of achievement and supports inspiration.

2. **Natural Inspiration:**
   While outer inspirations, for example, tasteful objectives or social endorsement can give starting stimulus, developing characteristic inspiration is a vital component in fostering serious areas of strength for a for wellness. Inherent inspiration originates from a veritable energy for the actual exercises, cultivating a feasible and pleasant way to deal with work out. Interfacing wellness objectives to individual qualities, like wellbeing, imperativeness, or a feeling of achievement, upgrades the characteristic inspiration that powers long haul responsibility.

3. **Positive Self-Talk and Assertions:**
   The language we use inside shapes our discernments and impacts our ways of behaving. Positive self-talk and confirmations assume a vital part in encouraging areas of strength for a for wellness. Changing negative contemplations into helpful confirmations can alleviate self-uncertainty and improve self-viability. Developing a propensity for empowering self-talk establishes a psychological climate helpful for tirelessness and strength notwithstanding challenges.

4. **Embracing the Development Outlook:**
   The idea of a development outlook, as proposed by clinician Tune Dweck, stresses the conviction that capacities and insight can be created through devotion and difficult work. Applying the standards of a development mentality to wellness includes seeing difficulties as any open doors for development, embracing the expectation to learn and adapt, and understanding that mishaps are important for the excursion. This outlook shift cultivates strength and a readiness to continue even with challenges.

5. **Representation Procedures:**
   Representation is an integral asset that outfits the brain's capacity to make mental pictures of progress. Competitors and wellness aficionados frequently use perception strategies to intellectually practice their exercises, imagine accomplishing their objectives, and beat hindrances. Imagining the ideal results upgrades inspiration, hones center, and imparts a feeling of trust in one's capacity to succeed.

6. **Building Predictable Propensities:**
   The improvement of a solid outlook in wellness is intently attached to the foundation of steady propensities. Propensities, when imbued, become programmed ways of behaving that require less mental exertion. Making a normal that incorporates practice flawlessly into day to day existence cultivates discipline and limits choice weakness. Consistency in propensities adds to the improvement of

a versatile outlook by building up the idea that wellness is a non-debatable piece of one's way of life.

7. **Care and Presence:**
The act of care includes being completely present in the ongoing second without judgment. Coordinating care into wellness schedules elevates familiarity with substantial sensations,
improves the psyche body association, and advances a feeling of satisfaction in the current experience. Careful activity develops an appreciation for the cycle as opposed to focusing exclusively on ultimate objectives, encouraging a positive and feasible mentality.

8. **Acknowledgment of Defect:**
Hairsplitting can be an impediment to fostering areas of strength for a for wellness. Embracing the blemishes inborn in any wellness venture, recognizing mishaps without self-analysis, and understanding that progress is non-straight add to a more versatile outlook. Gaining from botches, changing course when important, and keeping a merciful demeanor toward oneself are critical parts of a versatile mentality.

9. **Responsibility and Emotionally supportive networks:**
The excursion to wellness is much of the time more practical and charming when embraced with an emotionally supportive network. Responsibility, whether through an exercise mate, a mentor, or a local area, gives outer inspiration and support. Sharing objectives, progress, and difficulties with others encourages a feeling of association and responsibility, building up the obligation to wellness goals.

10. **Versatility and Adaptability:**
Life is dynamic, and unexpected conditions might disturb wellness schedules. Fostering areas of strength for an includes developing versatility and adaptability notwithstanding change. Instead of review disturbances as unrealistic impediments, taking on a mentality that looks for elective arrangements and embraces flexibility upgrades strength and keeps difficulties from crashing progress.

11. **Observing Accomplishments, Of all shapes and sizes:**
Recognizing and commending accomplishments, whether they are significant achievements or little triumphs, is a critical part of keeping up with inspiration and building up a positive outlook. Festivities make a positive criticism circle, delivering dopamine and supporting the cerebrum's relationship among exertion and prize. Perceiving progress, regardless of how steady, adds to a feeling of achievement and powers proceeded with responsibility.

12. **Periodization and Rest:**
Overtraining and burnout can subvert the improvement of a solid outlook. Integrating times of rest and recuperation into wellness schedules is fundamental for long haul supportability. Periodization, the essential preparation of preparing cycles, considers variety in force and volume, forestalling physical and mental

weakness. Perceiving the significance of rest as a part of the general wellness system encourages a fair and versatile outlook.

13. **Gaining from Difficulties:**
Difficulties are unavoidable in any wellness venture, and the capacity to gain from them is a sign of major areas of strength for a. As opposed to review misfortunes as disappointments, they can be reexamined as any open doors for development and learning.

Investigating the elements that prompted a difficulty, changing the methodology, and applying newly discovered information add to a versatile outlook that explores difficulties with flexibility and a feeling of direction.

14. **Persistent Learning and Interest:**
Moving toward wellness with an outlook of persistent learning and interest encourages a continuous feeling of commitment and energy. Looking for new activities, investigating different wellness modalities, and remaining informed about the most recent exploration in practice science add to a powerful mentality. The ability to learn and adjust improves the viability of wellness schedules as well as forestalls dullness and weariness.

15. **Intelligent Practices:**

Normal reflection on the wellness venture gives a valuable chance to evaluate progress, reevaluate objectives, and recognize regions for development. Journaling, self-evaluation, and careful reflection add to mindfulness and a more profound comprehension of the mental parts of wellness. Intelligent practices permit people to follow their outlook, commend victories, and make informed changes in accordance with their wellness approach.

In the complex embroidery of wellness, the improvement of a solid outlook arises as a dynamic and continuous cycle. The procedures illustrated above are not separated techniques but rather interconnected strings that, when woven together, make a tough and versatile mentality. The coordination of these mental techniques into the texture of one's way to deal with wellness adds to an all encompassing and maintainable outlook that rises above transient objectives, cultivating a deep rooted obligation to prosperity.

As people leave on their wellness processes, the development of a solid outlook turns into an extraordinary power that stretches out past actual results. It shapes perspectives, convictions, and propensities, impacting how people approach practice as well as how they explore difficulties, misfortunes, and the more extensive scene of their lives. In the blend of physical and mental prosperity, a solid outlook fills in as the compass that guides people toward a way of persevering through wellbeing, essentialness, and satisfaction.

2.3 Setting realistic expectations and cultivating a positive mental attitude

Chasing individual and expert development, setting reasonable assumptions and developing a positive mental demeanor arise as primary rules that shape the direction of one's excursion. The sensitive interchange between these two angles shapes the bedrock whereupon people fabricate strength, explore difficulties, and embrace the intrinsic back and forth movement of life. This investigation digs into the mental subtleties behind setting feasible assumptions and cultivating a positive outlook, enlightening the harmonious connection between the two.

Reasonable Assumptions:

Setting reasonable assumptions includes a nuanced comprehension of one's capacities, the setting of the undertaking, and the inescapable vulnerabilities that go with any pursuit. Ridiculous assumptions can prompt dissatisfaction, disappointment, and a feeling of disappointment, while grounded assumptions add to a better and more maintainable way to deal with objective setting.

1. **Mindfulness and Evaluation:**
   An essential beginning stage in setting sensible assumptions is developing mindfulness. This includes a real evaluation of one's assets, constraints, and the variables that might impact the ideal result. Grasping one's abilities, information, and current limits gives a practical establishment whereupon to construct assumptions. Recognizing regions that require advancement or improvement encourages a productive way to deal with objective setting.

2. **Thought of Outside Variables:**
   Sensible assumptions consider the outside factors that might influence the excursion toward an objective. Outer impacts, like monetary circumstances, cultural standards, or startling life altering situations, can influence the speed and result of tries. By taking into account these variables, people can integrate adaptability into their assumptions, considering transformation and versatility even with unanticipated conditions.

3. **Gradual Advancement and Achievements:**
   Separating bigger objectives into more modest, sensible achievements adds to a reasonable and feasible system. Steady advancement gives a feeling of achievement as well as takes into consideration progressing changes in view of criticism and experience. Praising these more modest triumphs supports inspiration and builds up a positive input circle, improving the probability of supported exertion and responsibility.

4. **Arrangement with Values and Needs:**
   Sensible assumptions are moored in a reasonable comprehension of individual qualities and needs. Objectives that line up with one's guiding principle and general life needs are bound to be sought after with commitment and excitement. Assessing the meaning of an objective inside the more extensive setting of one's life guarantees that the pursuit is significant and thunderous, adding to a manageable and positive outlook.

5. **Gaining from Misfortunes:**
   Reasonable assumptions recognize the certainty of difficulties and difficulties. As opposed to survey misfortunes as outlandish disappointments, they are viewed as necessary pieces of the growing experience. Embracing an outlook that sees difficulties as any open doors for development and refinement cultivates strength and flexibility. Gaining from mishaps permits people to change assumptions, refine systems, and persevere with a feeling of direction.
6. **Adaptability and Flexibility:**
   The capacity to adjust and stay adaptable even with changing conditions is a sign of reasonable assumptions. Life is dynamic, and unexpected occasions might require acclimations to the first arrangement. Developing adaptability permits people to explore unforeseen turns with a positive outlook, perceiving that flexibility is a strength instead of a split the difference.
7. **Adjusted Good faith:**

Practical assumptions find some kind of harmony among confidence and realism. While confidence powers inspiration and an uplifting perspective, it should be tempered with a practical comprehension of expected difficulties and vulnerabilities. Adjusted hopefulness recognizes the chance of progress while getting ready for the innate troubles that might emerge en route.

Developing a Positive Mental Demeanor:
A positive mental demeanor is an extraordinary power that shapes insights, impacts ways of behaving, and adds to generally speaking prosperity. Developing this disposition includes deliberate practices that cultivate idealism, flexibility, and a useful way to deal with life's difficulties.

1. **Appreciation Practices:**
   Appreciation is an intense device for developing a positive mental demeanor. Routinely offering thanks for parts of life, both of all shapes and sizes, moves the concentration toward positive components. Keeping an appreciation diary, pondering positive encounters, and recognizing the commitments of others add to an outlook that values the overflow throughout everyday life.
2. **Care and Present Second Mindfulness:**
   Care rehearses, like reflection and careful breathing, anchor people right now. Developing familiarity with the present diminishes nervousness about the future and second thoughts about the past. Care encourages a positive mental demeanor by advancing a non-critical acknowledgment of the ongoing experience and an appreciation for the extravagance of every second.
3. **Positive Self-Talk and Certifications:**
   The language we use inside shapes our insights and impacts our feelings. Positive self-talk includes supplanting negative or self-decisive considerations with

confirming and useful explanations. Insistences, rehashed positive explanations, build up a positive outlook by establishing a psychological climate that upholds self-conviction and good faith.

4. **Strength Building:**
A positive mental disposition is intently attached to strength — the capacity to return from misfortune. Flexibility building rehearses include reevaluating difficulties as any open doors, creating survival methods, and survey misfortunes as impermanent as opposed to long-lasting.
Embracing mishaps as a component of the excursion cultivates a mentality that sees challenges as conquerable and safe.

5. **Encircling Oneself with Inspiration:**
Individuals, conditions, and media we encircle ourselves with essentially influence our psychological demeanor. Developing positive connections, investing energy in elevating conditions, and being aware of media utilization add to a positive mental standpoint. Keeping away from harmful impacts and effectively looking for energy in different parts of life improves in general prosperity.

6. **Objective Representation:**
Representation is a useful asset for encouraging a positive mental demeanor. Envisioning the fruitful acknowledgment of objectives, imagining the excursion with clear detail, and encountering the feelings related with accomplishment add to a good outlook. Objective representation upgrades inspiration, supports responsibility, and gives a psychological outline to progress.

7. **Thoughtful gestures and Liberality:**
Taking part in thoughtful gestures and liberality toward others proportionally affects one's own psychological disposition. Helping other people, communicating benevolence, and participating in philanthropic activities add to a positive feeling of direction and association. Thoughtful gestures benefit beneficiaries as well as improve the provider's general feeling of prosperity and energy.

8. **Learning and Development Outlook:**
A positive mental demeanor is interwoven with a development outlook — the conviction that capacities and insight can be created through exertion and learning. Embracing difficulties as any open doors for development, looking for consistent learning, and reevaluating disappointments as venturing stones to progress cultivate an outlook that blossoms with progress and flexibility.

9. **Alliance with Strong People group:**
Having a place with steady networks gives a feeling of association, common perspective, and shared support. Whether in private or expert circles, affiliating with networks that elevate and uphold cultivates a positive mental demeanor. Shared encounters, aggregate objectives, and a feeling of having a place add to a hopeful and valuable mentality.

10. **Taking care of oneself Practices:**
Dealing with one's physical and mental prosperity is fundamental to keeping an

uplifting outlook. Satisfactory rest, standard activity, sound nourishment, and practices that elevate unwinding add to in general prosperity. At the point when the body is supported, the psyche is stronger, hopeful, and better prepared to explore life's difficulties.
11. **Assertion of Individual Qualities:**
Perceiving and insisting individual qualities adds to a positive mental demeanor. Recognizing accomplishments, communicating trust in one's capacities, and celebrating individual qualities cultivate a mentality that values individual versatility and capability. This confirmation of qualities supports confidence and adds to a hopeful standpoint.
12. **Useful Critical thinking:**
A positive mental disposition is intently attached to the capacity to move toward difficulties with a helpful critical thinking outlook. As opposed to harping on issues, people with an inspirational perspective spotlight on arrangements. They view provokes as any open doors to practice imagination, strength, and versatility, encouraging a feeling of strengthening notwithstanding troubles.
13. **Development of Hopeful Reasoning Examples:**
Hopeful reasoning includes seeing circumstances from a perspective that underscores positive results and conceivable outcomes. Developing hopeful reasoning examples includes testing negative considerations, reexamining troubles as conquerable, and zeroing in on the potential for positive change. Hopeful reasoning adds to a positive mental demeanor by forming discernments and understandings of occasions.
14. **Intelligent Practices:**

Standard reflection on one's viewpoints, feelings, and encounters adds to the development of a good mental disposition. Journaling, self-evaluation, and careful reflection give experiences into thought processes and regions for development. Intelligent practices upgrade mindfulness and add to the continuous refinement of a positive mentality.

In the harmonious dance between setting sensible assumptions and developing a positive mental disposition, people weave an embroidery of versatility, hopefulness, and reason. Reasonable assumptions ground goals in reasonableness, encouraging a pride and forestalling disappointment. All the while, a positive mental disposition mixes the excursion with euphoria, imagination, and an unflinching faith in the potential for development and satisfaction.

As people explore the intricacies of their own and proficient lives, the joining of reasonable assumptions and a positive mental demeanor turns into a dynamic and extraordinary power. It shapes the focal point through which difficulties are seen, impacts the systems utilized to conquer snags, and eventually decides the versatility and satisfaction got from the excursion. In the association of these two support points, people track down a decent and versatile way to deal with the consistently developing scene of their desires and attempts.

Chapter 3

The Anvil of Discipline

In the huge territory of the vast embroidery, where the strings of existence entwine, there exists a domain known as the Iron block of Discipline. It is a spot past the bounds of standard comprehension, a pot where the substance of character is produced and tempered. Inside its ethereal limits, the reverberations of assurance and the clangor of resolve resonate through the ages.

The Iron block is definitely not an actual substance, yet a magical develop that rises above the constraints of mortal discernment. It exists in the domain of goals, where the unrefined substance of potential is molded into the persevering through type of trained strength. The individuals who adventure into this magical fashion do so energetically, for they look for the extraordinary power that main the Iron block can present.

The excursion to the Iron block is definitely not a simple one. It requires a profound contemplation, an eagerness to face one's inward devils, and a promise to personal development. Many flounder on the way, unfit to endure the burning intensity of self-assessment or the heaviness of their own weaknesses. In any case, for the people who continue on, the prizes are unmatched.

As one methodologies the Iron block, the air becomes accused of an obvious energy. The actual texture of reality appears to sparkle with potential, and the scene transforms into a strange scene of conceptual structures and moving varieties. It is where the limits among thought and substance obscure, and the psyche overshadows the material.

In this ethereal domain, the Blacksmith's iron itself is a sign of discipline — an epic design of glimmering powerful metal, suspended in the void. Its surface is carved with the endless accounts of the individuals who have preceded, their battles and wins perpetually engraved upon the substance of the Blacksmith's iron. As rookies step into its closeness, they become piece of this continuous adventure, contributing their own story to the amazing embroidery of discipline.

The Iron block requests reflection. It expects people to defy their shortcomings, recognize their imperfections, and embrace the potential for development. It's anything but a spot for weak willed or those reluctant to dive into the openings of their own mind. The Iron block is a mirror that mirrors the real essence of the people who stand before it, stripping away the facade of self-misdirection and uncovering the center of their being.

In this cauldron of self-revelation, people are gone up against with their decisions and the results of their activities. Each choice, each dithering, and each win is revealed for assessment. It is a course of stripping away the layers of misrepresentation and defying the unvarnished reality of one's personality.

The Iron block is apathetic regarding pardons. It doesn't respect the legitimizations and avocations that people use to safeguard themselves from responsibility. All things being equal, it requests a retribution — an affirmation of obligation regarding one's own decisions and a promise to redress previous mishaps. It is where the cauldron of outcome meets the mallet of responsibility, producing a purpose that can endure the everyday hardships.

As people explore the confounded halls of the Blacksmith's iron, they experience reverberations of the past — murmurs of the individuals who have confronted comparative preliminaries and arisen more grounded for it. These ghastly voices act as the two aides and admonitions, offering experiences into the traps that lie ahead and the temperances that can prompt victory. The Iron block is a storehouse of aggregate insight, a supply of information refined from the encounters of endless spirits.

The excursion through the Iron block is certainly not a single undertaking. The people who navigate its supernatural territory frequently end up in the organization of others, individual searchers on an equal way of self-disclosure. The bonds manufactured in the cauldron of the Blacksmith's iron are significant, rising above the limits of existence. Together, people backing and challenge one another, filling in as mirrors that mirror the qualities and shortcomings of their mates.

In the core of the Blacksmith's iron, there lies an office of preliminaries — a pot inside the cauldron. Here, people are exposed to trial of their backbone, provokes that push them as far as possible and then some. These preliminaries are not erratic; they are custom-made to every person, intended to target explicit parts of character and uncover regions needing refinement.

The preliminaries are not without reason. They act as impetuses for development, open doors for people to defy their feelings of trepidation and beaten their impediments. Every preliminary is a figurative mallet blow, molding the natural substance of potential into a versatile and persevering through structure. The people who rise up out of these preliminaries are not solid, however they bear the signs of their encounters like symbols of honor.

One of the focal principles of the Iron block is the development of discipline — a quality that rises above simple discretion and reaches out to the domain of dominance. Discipline is the cauldron through which crude potential is changed into persevering through strength. The power permits people to drive forward despite difficulty, to stick to their standards when stood up to with enticement, and to fashion a way of direction and significance.

Discipline is certainly not an inflexible adjustment to outer standards; it is a dynamic and incorporated set of rules. It is the capacity to remain consistent with one's qualities and responsibilities, even without any outside oversight. In the Blacksmith's iron, people discover that discipline is certainly not a one-time accomplishment yet a continuous cycle — an excursion of steady refinement and personal development.

The Iron block instructs that discipline is definitely not a single undertaking yet a shared exertion. The bonds fashioned between people in the pot of the Blacksmith's iron make an organization of help and responsibility. In this interconnected web, people draw strength from one another, giving consolation in the midst of battle and praising triumphs together. The Iron block is a demonstration of the possibility that the strength of the individual is indistinguishable from the strength of the local area.

As people progress through the Blacksmith's iron, they come to understand that discipline is definitely not a static state yet a unique balance. It requires consistent cautiousness and transformation to evolving conditions.

The Blacksmith's iron is a living element that develops alongside the people who occupy its magical scope. In this steadily moving scene, people figure out how to embrace change and explore the unusual flows of existence with strength and reason.

The Iron block additionally bestows the insight that discipline isn't inseparable from unbending nature. There's actually no need to focus on smothering inventiveness or stifling uniqueness. All things being equal, discipline gives the structure inside which inventiveness can prosper and singularity can track down its actual articulation. The trained brain is an adaptable psyche, equipped for adjusting to new difficulties and tracking down creative arrangements.

In the Iron block, people come to comprehend that discipline isn't an objective yet an excursion — a persistent taking a stab at greatness and discipline. The Blacksmith's iron isn't where one accomplishes flawlessness; it is where one sharpens the devices vital for the continuous quest for flawlessness. The excursion through the Iron block is a repetitive course of development, challenge, and refinement that rehashes all through a lifetime.

The Blacksmith's iron of Discipline isn't restricted to a particular time or spot. It exists in the everlasting present, an immortal domain where past, present, and future combine. The individuals who leave on the excursion through the Blacksmith's iron end up associated with a genealogy of searchers that stretches across the ages. They become piece of a living custom, contributing their own section to the continuous story of discipline.

In the Blacksmith's iron, people encounter the idea of heritage. They wrestle with the possibility that their activities and decisions resonate past the limits of their nearby presence. The Iron block instructs that the heritage one leaves isn't estimated in material abundance or outside awards however in the effect one has on the existences of others and the engraving one leaves on the shared awareness.

The Iron block moves people to rise above the fleeting and embrace the persevering. It calls them to transcend the transient interruptions of the material world and spotlight on the timeless rules that shape character and characterize reason. In the Iron block, people go up against the fleetingness of life and find the immortal pith that lives inside.

As people explore the last phases of their excursion through the Iron block, they arise changed — manufactured in the cauldron of discipline, tempered by the preliminaries of character, and saturated with the insight of the ages. They convey with them the permanent characteristics of their encounters, carved into the actual texture of their being. The Blacksmith's iron doesn't guarantee a simple way, however it offers a significant and getting through change for the people who try to step its supernatural hallways.

Eventually, the Iron block of Discipline is a figurative scene — an emblematic portrayal of the inside and outer difficulties that people face on their journey for self-discipline. A demonstration of the thought genuine strength isn't brought into the world of solace and simplicity however is produced in the cauldron of misfortune. The Blacksmith's iron is a greeting — an encouragement to leave on an excursion of self-revelation, to stand up to the shadows inside, and to rise up out of the cauldron with a restrained heart and a getting through soul.

As the reverberations of the Iron block resound through the passageways of time, they act as a wake up call that the excursion of discipline is continuous. It is an unending journey for development, a persistent quest for greatness, and a pledge to a better quality of living. The Iron block of Discipline entices to all who look to produce their personality in the flames of self-revelation, welcoming them to embrace the groundbreaking power that exists in the cauldron of discipline.

3.1 Understanding the role of discipline in building a steel physique

In the domain of actual wellness and lifting weights, discipline is a vital foundation that establishes the groundwork for a steel constitution. It is the immovable obligation to an organized routine of preparing, nourishment, and way of life that changes the human body into a chiseled magnum opus of muscle and strength. Understanding the job of discipline in this pursuit isn't only a hypothetical activity; a reasonable and extraordinary excursion requires devotion, strength, and a profound appreciation for the cooperative connection among exertion and result.

At its center, discipline with regards to lifting weights is about adherence to a bunch of rules that oversee each part of the wellness venture. It envelops the predictable execution of exercises, the fastidious administration of dietary admission, and the development of propensities that help the overall objective of actual change. Discipline is the planner that plans the outline for a steel constitution and the designer that manages the development of each muscle fiber and ligament.

The discipline expected for building a steel physical make-up reaches out past the bounds of the rec center. It pervades each aspect of life, impacting day to day decisions and ways of behaving. Sustenance, rest, stress the executives, and generally way of life become basic parts of the discipline condition. The weight lifter's process isn't compartmentalized; a comprehensive undertaking perceives the interconnectedness of physical, mental, and close to home prosperity.

In the pot of discipline, the primary component to be formed is the gym routine. Consistency is the key part of progress in working out, and discipline guarantees that every meeting is drawn nearer with reason and commitment. The restrained muscle head sticks to a very much organized preparing plan, adjusting obstruction preparing, cardiovascular activity, and adaptability work. The obligation to routineness in preparing is non-debatable, and deviations from the arrangement are seen as obstacles to advance.

The trained muscle head figures out the significance of moderate over-burden, persistently moving the body to adjust and develop. The loads lifted, the quantity of reiterations performed, and the power of every exercise are fastidiously followed and changed over the long run. Discipline in the rec center isn't simply about making a cursory effort; it is tied in with stretching boundaries, breaking levels, and embracing the distress that goes with development.

Sustenance is the second mainstay of discipline chasing a steel constitution. The trained muscle head perceives that the kitchen is just about as essential as the rec center in the chiseling system. Powering the body with the right supplements in the right extents is a science that expects tender loving care and an essential methodology. Trained nourishment includes exact caloric admission, macronutrient dissemination, and dinner timing.

Feast readiness turns into a custom for the restrained muscle head, with every piece of food filling a particular need chasing ideal physical make-up structure. The restrained way to deal with sustenance goes past the charm of craze diets or brief limitations. It is a reasonable and adjusted approach to eating that upholds the requests of serious preparation and works with recuperation. The trained weight lifter comprehends that sustenance is definitely not a momentary fix yet a deep rooted obligation to wellbeing and execution.

Past the rec center and the kitchen, discipline penetrates the way of life decisions of the muscle head. Satisfactory and quality rest is focused on, perceiving its part in recuperation, hormonal equilibrium, and in general prosperity. Stress the board turns into a cognizant practice, as stress chemicals can block progress and sabotage the body's capacity to adjust to preparing upgrades. The restrained weight lifter develops propensities that add to the enhancement of physical and emotional wellness.

Chasing a steel body, discipline turns into a psychological mentality as much as a social quality. The trained brain is engaged, tough, and equipped for enduring the difficulties innate in the groundbreaking excursion. A mentality sees mishaps as any open doors for learning, hindrances as venturing stones, and distress as a fundamental friend making a course for significance.

The restrained weight lifter isn't influenced by the appeal of alternate routes or handy solutions. The market is loaded with commitments of fast changes through supplements, sketchy dietary practices, or untested preparation strategies. Notwithstanding, the restrained individual comprehends that feasible advancement is the aftereffect of steady exertion after some time. There are no enchanted pills or mystery recipes; there is just the restrained execution of demonstrated standards.

The job of discipline reaches out to the close to home domain also. Building a steel constitution isn't without difficulties and disappointments. Levels, wounds, and snapshots of self-question are unavoidable.

The trained weight lifter moves toward these difficulties with an unemotional purpose, understanding that the way to progress is certainly not a straight direction. Discipline is the anchor that keeps debilitation from crashing the excursion and the compass that focuses the way forward.

The restrained muscle head is likewise receptive to the mental parts of the physical make-up change process. Self-perception, confidence, and the development of a positive outlook are vital parts of the discipline condition. The trained individual perceives that the quest for a steel constitution isn't exclusively about actual appearance yet includes a comprehensive way to deal with personal development and self-strengthening.

In the realm of weight training, discipline is definitely not an unbending and severe power however a freeing and enabling one. The partner gives construction and request to the tumultuous and requesting nature of the extraordinary excursion. The trained weight lifter doesn't see discipline as a penance yet as a venture — a cognizant decision to focus on long haul prosperity and the satisfaction of individual potential.

The job of discipline in working out turns out to be especially obvious during times of affliction. Wounds, ailments, or life's startling difficulties can crash progress and test the determination of even the most committed people. The trained jock, in any case, moves toward these difficulties with an essential mentality. Changes are made to preparing conventions, sustenance is adjusted to oblige evolving conditions, and the restrained soul stays whole.

The excursion to a steel build is definitely not a singular one. Discipline cultivates a feeling of local area and kinship among similar people who share a similar enthusiasm for personal development. The restrained jock perceives the worth of an encouraging group of people — whether it be preparing accomplices, mentors, or the more extensive wellness local area. The trading of information, support, and shared encounters upgrades the excursion and builds up the discipline that supports it.

The trained quest for a steel body isn't restricted to a particular age, orientation, or foundation. It is a comprehensive and engaging undertaking that rises above cultural generalizations and assumptions. The discipline expected is a general rule that applies to anybody focused on the quest for actual greatness. The rec center turns into a mixture of variety, where people from varying backgrounds meet in their common commitment to the groundbreaking excursion.

In the scene of working out, discipline additionally stretches out to the moral component of the game. The trained muscle head sticks to standards of decency, respectability, and sportsmanship. The utilization of execution improving substances, restricted substances, or deceptive practices is contradictory to the soul of discipline. The quest for a steel physical make-up isn't a reason for undermining one's trustworthiness; it is a chance to epitomize the best expectations of character.

The job of discipline in working out isn't restricted to the singular level; it stretches out to the more extensive cultural view of wellness and constitution change. The trained weight lifter turns into an envoy for the positive parts of a sound and restrained way of life. Dispersing fantasies, testing generalizations, and advancing a decent and proof based way to deal with wellness add to the rise of the whole wellness local area.

All in all, understanding the job of discipline in building a steel body goes past the superficial impression of actual feel. It digs into the complex exchange of steady exertion, vital preparation, and a comprehensive way to deal with prosperity. Discipline is certainly not a prohibitive power however a freeing one — a core value that enables people to assume command over their physical, mental, and profound wellbeing.

The trained jock is a demonstration of the groundbreaking force of centered exertion and unfaltering responsibility. Through the pot of discipline, the human body turns into a living figure — a demonstration of the unstoppable soul and the boundless potential that dwells inside. The excursion to a steel constitution isn't an objective however a persistent development — a ceaseless journey for personal growth, self-disclosure, and the acknowledgment of one's maximum capacity.

3.2 Strategies for creating and maintaining healthy habits

In the maze of day to day existence, where horde decisions and interruptions proliferate, the quest for wellbeing is frequently much the same as exploring a complicated labyrinth. In the midst of the whirlwind of obligations, enticements, and time limitations, the foundation and propagation of solid propensities arise as vital foundations of prosperity. Procedures for making and keeping up with these propensities require a mix of aim, care, and a far reaching comprehension of the variables that impact conduct. This investigation dives into the complexities of developing and supporting solid propensities as a groundbreaking excursion toward enduring imperativeness.

At the core of any undertaking to encourage solid propensities lies the meaning of purposefulness. A cognizant choice to focus on wellbeing and prosperity is the impetus that starts the course of propensity development. Deliberateness includes a promise to change, an acknowledgment of the worth that wellbeing holds in the excellent embroidery of life. Without an unmistakable goal, propensities risk being random or transitory, powerless to the impulses of situation as opposed to moored in a purposeful decision for enduring change.

To set out on the way of sound propensity development, characterizing clear and reachable goals is fundamental. These objectives act as directing lights, giving an internal compass and inspiration. Whether the point is to consolidate customary activity, take on a nutritious eating routine, further develop rest quality, or oversee pressure really, explicitness in objective setting upgrades the lucidity of the way forward. The restrained quest for clear cut targets adjusts activities to reason, changing dubious goals into unmistakable achievements.

A vital part of making solid propensities is figuring out the force of steady advancement. The excursion toward ideal wellbeing isn't a run yet a long distance race — a steady and supported exertion. Little, predictable advances structure the structure blocks of enduring propensities. By separating bigger objectives into reasonable undertakings, people lessen the apparent weight of progress and make a feeling of achievement with each step in the right direction. This approach cultivates a positive criticism circle, building up the conviction that progress is feasible and practical.

Much the same as a painter carefully making a show-stopper, the plan of the climate assumes a vital part in molding propensities. The physical and social environmental factors can either work with or upset the foundation of sound schedules. Building a climate that prods conduct toward positive decisions includes vital alterations. For example, setting sound tidbits inside simple reach, coordinating exercise gear noticeably, or developing a group of friends that urges wellbeing all add to a climate helpful for solid propensities.

The idea of propensity stacking includes incorporating new ways of behaving into existing schedules. By partner another propensity with a laid out one, people influence the energy of existing practices to flawlessly present positive changes. This procedure profits by the mind's proclivity for examples and schedules, making brain associations that interface the new propensity to a laid out sign or custom. Propensity stacking changes the development of sound propensities into a cooperative interaction that piggybacks on existing examples of conduct.

In the computerized age, where innovation is ubiquitous, saddling its true capacity turns into a powerful system for propensity development. Portable applications, wearable gadgets, and online stages offer apparatuses that work with objective following, give updates, and deal bits of knowledge into progress. The mix of innovation into the quest for sound propensities adds a component of responsibility and straightforwardness, transforming cell phones and smartwatches into individual health associates.

The development of care arises as a key part in the creation and upkeep of solid propensities. Care includes an uplifted consciousness of the current second, an attunement to contemplations, feelings, and actual sensations. By rehearsing care, people gain understanding into the triggers and prompts that impact their way of behaving. This mindfulness turns into an integral asset for perceiving and diverting routine reactions, cultivating a cognizant and purposeful way to deal with everyday decisions.

A pivotal component in the excursion toward solid propensities is figuring out the mental underpinnings of conduct. The propensity circle — containing a sign, everyday practice, and prize — is a structure that clarifies the recurrent idea of propensities.

Recognizing the signals that trigger bothersome propensities, supplanting pointless schedules with better other options, and guaranteeing a satisfying prize framework are essential moves toward overhauling the propensity circle. This mental methodology changes propensity development from a clash of self control into a key and informed process.

Social elements use significant impact over individual way of behaving. Utilizing the force of local area and social help becomes instrumental in supporting sound propensities. Whether through exercise mates, responsibility accomplices, or cooperation in bunch exercises, the aggregate energy of a steady local area encourages inspiration and flexibility. Shared objectives and common consolation make a feeling of having a place, changing the quest for wellbeing into a common excursion.

In the midst of the heap interruptions competing for focus in present day life, using time effectively arises as a basic procedure for propensity development. Focusing on wellbeing requires a proactive distribution of time for exercises like activity, dinner planning, and taking care of oneself. The trained administration of time includes defining limits, dispensing with time-squandering exercises, and perceiving that the interest in wellbeing is a promise to long haul prosperity.

While leaving on the excursion of propensity arrangement, people experience unavoidable misfortunes and difficulties. A strong outlook, portrayed by a positive reaction to misfortune, is a powerful system for exploring impediments. As opposed to survey mishaps as disappointments, embracing a development outlook sees them as any open doors for learning and refinement. This psychological strength is a powerful power that changes mishaps into venturing stones, bracing the obligation to sound propensities.

A foundation of propensity development is the development of self-sympathy. Recognizing that flawlessness is an impossible norm, people embrace self-sympathy as an offset to self-analysis. Self-sympathy includes treating oneself with graciousness, perceiving the common mankind of confronting difficulties, and understanding that mishaps are intrinsic in the excursion toward positive change. This sustaining approach makes a genuinely strong starting point for manageable propensity arrangement.

The study of propensity development highlights the significance of reiteration and consistency. Propensities are built up through reiteration, as predictable way of behaving makes brain processes that become progressively imbued. A promise to everyday consistency, even in little augmentations, moves the change of ways of behaving from cognizant decisions to programmed reactions. Redundancy turns into the cauldron in which propensities are produced, reshaping brain hardware and laying out persevering through examples of conduct.

The incorporation of reflection and assessment into the propensity development process adds an element of mindfulness and flexibility. Consistently evaluating progress, recognizing regions for development, and praising accomplishments add to a dynamic and iterative way to deal with propensity development. The propensity for reflection turns into a mirror that reflects self-awareness, directing people toward progressing refinement of their health process.

Finding some kind of harmony among adaptability and construction is essential in the creation and support of sound propensities. While structure gives the system to consistency and schedule, adaptability obliges the back and forth movement of life's unusualness. Perceiving that deviations from the arrangement are not inseparable from disappointment, however open doors for variation, imparts a feeling of versatility. The interchange among design and adaptability makes a supportable and versatile way to deal with propensity development.

A comprehensive way to deal with wellbeing incorporates actual prosperity as well as mental and close to home health. Incorporating rehearses that sustain mental and profound wellbeing — like care, reflection, and stress the executives — into the propensity development process makes a far reaching starting point for generally prosperity. The cooperative energy among physical and mental wellbeing changes the quest for solid propensities into an agreeable and coordinated venture.

In the domain of propensity development, the job of natural inspiration couldn't possibly be more significant. Inborn inspiration emerges from inner factors like individual qualities, real interest, and a feeling of independence. Developing propensities driven by natural inspiration rises above outer prizes or cultural assumptions. It takes advantage of the person's intrinsic longings and interests, encouraging a feeling of satisfaction that supports the force of propensity development.

The festival of achievements, both of all shapes and sizes, turns into a custom that builds up the positive parts of propensity development. Recognizing accomplishments, regardless of how steady, makes a feeling of achievement and spurs proceeded with exertion. The propensity for festivity pervades the excursion with happiness and fulfillment, highlighting the natural prizes inborn chasing after wellbeing.

As people navigate the multifaceted territory of propensity development, they understand that the excursion is definitely not a direct movement however a repeating and developing cycle. Propensities are dynamic substances that adjust to evolving conditions, encounters, and needs. Perceiving that the excursion is a continuous investigation as opposed to an objective cultivates a mentality of ceaseless development and development.

3.3 Overcoming common challenges and temptations

Leaving on an excursion of self-awareness and positive change is an estimable pursuit, yet it isn't without its portion of difficulties and enticements. The way to personal growth frequently meets with obstructions that test one's purpose and present the charm of recognizable, agreeable propensities. Conquering these normal difficulties requires a blend of mindfulness, vital preparation, and versatility. This investigation digs into the nuanced scene of self-improvement, offering bits of knowledge into how people can explore and win over the obstructions that might emerge on their extraordinary excursions.

One common test headed for self-awareness is the protection from change — a mental peculiarity profoundly imbued in the human mind. The solace of commonality and the anxiety toward the obscure make an impressive hindrance to venturing outside laid out safe places. Beating protection from change includes a change in outlook, reevaluating change as a chance for development as opposed to a danger to security.

Mindfulness turns into a signal in exploring the protection from change. Understanding the basic feelings of dread and convictions that add to obstruction permits people to straightforwardly address these elements. By recognizing and testing restricting convictions, people can make a psychological space helpful for change. The course of mindfulness includes thoughtfulness, reflection, and a legit assessment of the inspirations driving the longing for self-awareness.

Another normal test is the effect of outer impacts on one's excursion of personal growth. Prevalent burdens, cultural assumptions, and the impact of friend gatherings can apply a strong power that pulls against individual desires. Conquering these outside pressures requires an enduring obligation to validness and an unmistakable comprehension of one's qualities and needs.

Exploring outer impacts starts with laying out areas of strength for an of self and a profound association with individual qualities. At the point when people are grounded in their qualities, outside pressures hold less influence over their choices. Laying out sound limits and figuring out how to decisively impart one's necessities and yearnings to others are key techniques for conquering the outside powers that might ruin self-awareness.

Stalling, frequently energized by a feeling of dread toward disappointment or hairsplitting, represents a huge obstacle on the excursion to self-awareness. The propensity to defer activity or keep away from errands that add to development subverts progress and builds up a pattern of inaction. Beating hesitation includes destroying the hidden mental hindrances and taking on functional methodologies to start and support force.

Tending to delaying requires a mix of self-empathy and responsibility. Perceiving that flawlessness is a ridiculous norm and that misfortunes are essential for the growing experience cultivates a mentality of self-sympathy. At the same time, laying out clear objectives, breaking them into sensible errands, and making an organized arrangement give a guide to responsibility. The propensity for taking little, reliable advances, in any event, when inspiration is low, shapes a strong remedy to stalling.

The bait of moment satisfaction and the predominance of transient delights present one more typical test on the way of self-awareness. The satisfaction got from prompt extravagance frequently rivals the deferred rewards related with long haul objectives. Beating the draw of moment delight includes developing persistence, fostering a ground breaking point of view, and perceiving the persevering through worth of deferred rewards.

Drive control and the capacity to defer delight are abilities that can be sharpened through purposeful practice. Care, which includes being available at the time without surrendering to hasty responses, is an important device in beating the charm of prompt delights. Envisioning the drawn out advantages of supported exertion and reliably supporting the association between current activities and future results add to building the versatility expected to oppose moment delight.

An inescapable test on the excursion of self-awareness is the effect of self-uncertainty and negative self-talk. Incorporating a story of deficiency or capitulating to the inability to embrace success can disintegrate certainty and block progress. Defeating self-question requires a pledge to self-sympathy, the development of a development outlook, and the key revamping of negative idea designs.

Checking self-question starts with a cognizant work to challenge and reexamine negative considerations. The act of self-sympathy includes treating oneself with thoughtfulness and figuring out, particularly in snapshots of seen disappointment or misfortunes. Embracing a development outlook, which perspectives challenges as any open doors for learning and development, moves the concentration from natural capacities to the improvement of abilities through exertion and determination.

Feeling of dread toward judgment and the longing for outer approval frequently cast a shadow on the quest for self-awareness. The apprehension about being scrutinized or misjudged can smother realness and lead people to adjust to cultural assumptions. Defeating the feeling of dread toward judgment includes embracing weakness, focusing on credibility, and perceiving that outside approval is a temporary wellspring of satisfaction.

Embracing weakness requires an eagerness to be seen, heard, and saw even in snapshots of defect. The fortitude to communicate one's legitimate self, in spite of the anxiety toward judgment, cultivates a feeling of freedom and strengthening.

Moving the concentration from outer approval to inner approval includes perceiving and celebrating individual accomplishments and development, free of outside feelings.

An unobtrusive yet unavoidable test on the excursion of self-improvement is the peculiarity of self destructive behavior. Oblivious ways of behaving, frequently established in firmly established convictions or previous encounters, can subvert progress and block the acknowledgment of potential. Conquering destructive behavior requires a guarantee to self-revelation, an investigation of basic convictions, and an intentional work to reconstruct reckless examples.

Tending to behave destructively starts with an investigation of the convictions and stories that add to sabotaging one's endeavors. This course of self-revelation might include looking for the direction of guides, mentors, or emotional well-being experts who can give experiences and backing. Making a positive and engaging story around oneself, in light of qualities and capacities, turns into a fundamental component in beating self destructive behavior.

The time imperative, a pervasive test in the cutting edge world, frequently arises as a hindrance to self-awareness. Adjusting the requests of work, family, and different obligations can leave brief period and energy for personal growth pursuits. Beating the imperative of time includes vital prioritization, successful using time productively, and the acknowledgment that putting resources into self-improvement yields profits in different everyday issues.

Prioritization is a critical procedure for beating time requirements. By distinguishing and zeroing in on high-influence exercises that line up with individual objectives, people expand the viability of their time. Time usage abilities, like defining clear boundaries, making plans, and killing time-squandering exercises, upgrade efficiency and make space for self-awareness. The affirmation that little, reliable endeavors compound after some time builds up the comprehension that self-awareness is an excursion, not an objective.

In the domain of self-improvement, the quest for different objectives at the same time can become overpowering. The test of keeping up with balance and forestalling burnout is a common concern. Defeating the overpower includes key objective setting, powerful using time productively, and the development of strength. Perceiving the interconnectedness of various features of life and embracing an all encompassing way to deal with prosperity add to practical advancement.

Key objective putting forth includes focusing on objectives in view of their importance and adjusting them to general life values. Separating bigger objectives into reasonable errands and making a bit by bit plan improves clearness and decreases the feeling of overpower. The act of taking care of oneself, consolidating exercises that recharge physical, mental, and profound energy, turns into an essential component in keeping up with balance and forestalling burnout.

Chasing self-improvement, the correlation trap — a propensity to gauge oneself against others — can upset progress and disintegrate confidence. The predominance of virtual entertainment and the organized idea of online personas add to unreasonable norms and encourage insecurities. Defeating the examination trap includes developing self-empathy, zeroing in on individual advancement, and perceiving that everybody's process is extraordinary.

Developing self-sympathy includes treating oneself with benevolence and figuring out, particularly in snapshots of seen disappointment or misfortunes. Moving the concentration from outer benchmarks to interior development measurements permits people to see the value in their exceptional excursion. The act of appreciation, recognizing and celebrating individual accomplishments, fills in as an offset to the correlation trap, cultivating a positive and self-certifying outlook.

Chasing self-awareness, the compulsion to return to old propensities can be a considerable foe. The commonality and solace of laid out schedules, regardless of whether they are counterproductive, can apply a strong draw. Conquering the charm of old propensities includes a key and purposeful methodology, including the recognizable proof of triggers, the foundation of new schedules, and the development of flexibility.

Distinguishing triggers that immediate the re-visitation of old propensities is a urgent move toward defeating their charm. Whether set off by pressure, weariness, or explicit ecological signals, understanding the variables that speedy old propensities permits people to carry out preventive methodologies. The foundation of new, better schedules makes a positive other option and disturbs the programmed reaction related with old propensities. The development of versatility includes perceiving that mishaps are inescapable and seeing them as any open doors for learning and refinement.

The excursion of self-improvement is certainly not a segregated undertaking yet is impacted by the interconnectedness of different life areas. Defeating difficulties requires an incorporated and comprehensive methodology that recognizes the collaboration between physical, mental, and close to home prosperity. The acknowledgment that self-awareness is a progressing, iterative interaction encourages an outlook of versatility and ceaseless development.

Leaving on any excursion of personal development and self-awareness is an honorable pursuit, yet it isn't without its portion of difficulties and enticements. The way to self-advancement frequently meets with impediments that test one's purpose and present the charm of natural, agreeable propensities. Defeating these normal difficulties requires a mix of mindfulness, vital preparation, and flexibility. This investigation dives into the nuanced scene of self-improvement, offering bits of knowledge into how people can explore and win over the obstructions that might emerge on their groundbreaking processes.

One predominant test making a course for self-awareness is the protection from change — a mental peculiarity profoundly imbued in the human mind. The solace of commonality and the feeling of dread toward the obscure make an imposing obstruction to venturing outside laid out safe places. Defeating protection from change includes a change in mentality, reexamining change as a chance for development as opposed to a danger to security.

Mindfulness turns into a reference point in exploring the protection from change. Understanding the hidden feelings of trepidation and convictions that add to opposition permits people to straightforwardly address these variables. By recognizing and testing restricting convictions, people can make a psychological space helpful for change. The course of mindfulness includes thoughtfulness, reflection, and a fair assessment of the inspirations driving the craving for self-improvement.

Another normal test is the effect of outer impacts on one's excursion of personal growth. Prevailing difficulties, cultural assumptions, and the impact of friend gatherings can apply a strong power that pulls against individual yearnings. Beating these outer tensions requires an unfaltering obligation to legitimacy and an unmistakable comprehension of one's qualities and needs.

Exploring outer impacts starts with laying out areas of strength for an of self and a profound association with individual qualities. At the point when people are grounded in their qualities, outside pressures hold less influence over their choices. Laying out sound limits and figuring out how to self-assuredly impart one's requirements and yearnings to others are key techniques for defeating the outer powers that might ruin self-awareness.

Lingering, frequently powered by an anxiety toward disappointment or compulsiveness, represents a critical obstacle on the excursion to self-awareness. The inclination to defer activity or keep away from undertakings that add to development sabotages progress and supports a pattern of inaction. Beating dawdling includes destroying the fundamental mental hindrances and embracing down to earth methodologies to start and support energy.

Tending to dawdling requires a mix of self-empathy and responsibility. Perceiving that flawlessness is a ridiculous norm and that difficulties are essential for the educational experience cultivates an outlook of self-empathy. At the same time, laying out clear objectives, breaking them into sensible undertakings, and making an organized arrangement give a guide to responsibility. The propensity for taking little, steady advances, in any event, when inspiration is low, shapes a strong cure to delaying.

The draw of moment delight and the pervasiveness of transient joys present one more typical test on the way of self-improvement. The delight got from prompt extravagance frequently rivals the postponed rewards related with long haul objectives.

Defeating the draw of moment delight includes developing persistence, fostering a ground breaking viewpoint, and perceiving the getting through worth of deferred rewards.

Drive control and the capacity to defer satisfaction are abilities that can be sharpened through intentional practice. Care, which includes being available at the time without surrendering to hasty responses, is a significant device in defeating the charm of quick joys. Picturing the drawn out advantages of supported exertion and reliably building up the association between current activities and future results add to building the versatility expected to oppose moment delight.

An unavoidable test on the excursion of self-awareness is the effect of self-uncertainty and negative self-talk. Incorporating a story of deficiency or surrendering to the inability to embrace success can dissolve certainty and hinder progress. Beating self-question requires a pledge to self-empathy, the development of a development outlook, and the key reworking of negative idea designs.

Neutralizing self-question starts with a cognizant work to challenge and reevaluate negative considerations. The act of self-empathy includes treating oneself with graciousness and grasping, particularly in snapshots of seen disappointment or misfortunes. Embracing a development mentality, which perspectives challenges as any open doors for learning and development, moves the concentration from natural capacities to the improvement of abilities through exertion and steadiness.

Feeling of dread toward judgment and the longing for outer approval frequently cast a shadow on the quest for self-awareness. The apprehension about being reprimanded or misconstrued can smother validness and lead people to adjust to cultural assumptions. Beating the feeling of dread toward judgment includes embracing weakness, focusing on genuineness, and perceiving that outside approval is a brief wellspring of satisfaction.

Embracing weakness requires a readiness to be seen, heard, and saw even in snapshots of flaw. The boldness to communicate one's real self, notwithstanding the feeling of dread toward judgment, cultivates a feeling of freedom and strengthening. Moving the concentration from outer approval to inside approval includes perceiving and celebrating individual accomplishments and development, free of outside conclusions.

An unobtrusive yet inescapable test on the excursion of self-awareness is the peculiarity of destructive behavior. Oblivious ways of behaving, frequently established in firmly established convictions or previous encounters, can sabotage progress and block the acknowledgment of potential. Conquering self destructive behavior requires a promise to self-disclosure, an investigation of fundamental convictions, and a purposeful work to reinvent pointless examples.

Tending to behave destructively starts with an investigation of the convictions and accounts that add to subverting one's endeavors. This course of self-disclosure might include looking for the direction of guides, mentors, or emotional wellness experts who can give bits of knowledge and backing. Making a positive and enabling story around oneself, in view of qualities and capacities, turns into a central component in beating destructive behavior.

The time requirement, an omnipresent test in the cutting edge world, frequently arises as an obstruction to self-awareness. Adjusting the requests of work, family, and different obligations can leave brief period and energy for personal development pursuits. Defeating the requirement of time includes vital prioritization, powerful using time effectively, and the acknowledgment that putting resources into self-improvement yields profits in different everyday issues.

Prioritization is a critical procedure for defeating time limitations. By recognizing and zeroing in on high-influence exercises that line up with individual objectives, people amplify the viability of their time. Time usage abilities, like defining clear boundaries, making plans, and dispensing with time-squandering exercises, upgrade efficiency and make space for self-improvement. The affirmation that little, reliable endeavors compound over the long haul builds up the comprehension that self-improvement is an excursion, not an objective.

In the domain of self-improvement, the quest for numerous objectives all the while can become overpowering. The test of keeping up with balance and forestalling burnout is a predominant concern. Defeating the overpower includes vital objective setting, powerful using time effectively, and the development of versatility. Perceiving the interconnectedness of various features of life and taking on an all encompassing way to deal with prosperity add to supportable advancement.

Vital objective defining includes focusing on objectives in view of their importance and adjusting them to all-encompassing life values. Separating bigger objectives into reasonable errands and making a bit by bit plan upgrades clearness and decreases the feeling of overpower. The act of taking care of oneself, consolidating exercises that recharge physical, mental, and close to home energy, turns into an essential component in keeping up with balance and forestalling burnout.

Chasing self-awareness, the examination trap — an inclination to quantify oneself against others — can impede progress and disintegrate confidence. The predominance of virtual entertainment and the arranged idea of online personas add to ridiculous principles and cultivate serious insecurities. Conquering the examination trap includes developing self-empathy, zeroing in on individual advancement, and perceiving that everybody's process is special.

Developing self-sympathy includes treating oneself with thoughtfulness and grasping, particularly in snapshots of seen disappointment or misfortunes. Moving the concentration from outside benchmarks to inward development measurements permits people to see the value in their extraordinary excursion. The act of appreciation, recognizing and celebrating individual accomplishments, fills in as an offset to the examination trap, cultivating a positive and self-confirming outlook.

Chasing self-improvement, the impulse to return to old propensities can be an impressive enemy. The commonality and solace of laid out schedules, regardless of whether they are counterproductive, can apply a strong draw. Defeating the charm of old propensities includes a key and deliberate methodology, including the recognizable proof of triggers, the foundation of new schedules, and the development of versatility.

Chapter 4

Hammering Out Goals

In the huge scene of human life, the quest for objectives remains as a crucial main impetus, moving people and social orders forward. Objectives act as reference points, directing our undertakings, molding our predeterminations, and giving inspiration to our activities. The most common way of working out objectives, be that as it may, is certainly not an oversimplified one; it includes a nuanced transaction of vision, assurance, and flexibility.

At the center of objective setting lies the inherent human longing for progress and personal growth. From the earliest phases of civilization to the current day, people have tried to rise above their ongoing conditions and reach for new levels. This intrinsic tendency toward objective setting has been an impetus for development, investigation, and the development of social orders.

One of the essential difficulties in working out objectives is the requirement for lucidity of vision. Without an unmistakable comprehension of what one means to accomplish, the way ahead becomes cloudy and questionable. It is in the cauldron of reflection and self-revelation that people fashion a dream that resounds with their desires. Whether it be private desires, proficient pursuits, or public goals, the crystallization of a convincing vision turns into the north star that directs the excursion.

In the domain of self-awareness, the most common way of working out objectives frequently includes a profound jump into one's qualities, interests, and long haul goals. Putting forth significant and legitimate objectives expects people to strip back the layers of cultural assumptions and companion impacts, uncovering the center components that characterize their one of a kind personality. This contemplative excursion establishes the groundwork for objectives that are achievable as well as lined up with a person's credible self.

In the expert circle, associations wrestle with the test of adjusting individual and aggregate objectives. The fashioning of a common vision turns into a vital endeavor, expecting pioneers to express a convincing story that moves and prepares groups. The harmonization of individual desires with hierarchical targets is much the same as the sensitive craft of organizing an orchestra, where each instrument adds to the general congruity.

In any case, the simple enunciation of objectives, whether individual or authoritative, is nevertheless the underlying stroke of the sledge. The ensuing blows should be vital and intentional, molding the natural substance of goals into a substantial and feasible structure. Objective setting is certainly not a static undertaking; a powerful interaction requests intermittent reassessment and refinement.

The way toward accomplishing objectives is frequently loaded with impediments and unanticipated difficulties. Even with misfortune, the versatility to continue on and adjust is the smith's sledge that tempers the guts of objectives. A faithful obligation to the quest for targets, combined with an eagerness to course-address when essential, recognizes the individuals who just put forth objectives from the people who accomplish them.

Besides, the method involved with working out objectives requires a sensible evaluation of assets and limitations. Defining impossible objectives without a clearheaded evaluation of one's capacities and constraints is likened to building impractical plans. Objectives that are grounded in sober mindedness and an unmistakable comprehension of the landscape are bound to endure the everyday hardships and difficulty.

In the mind boggling embroidery of human connections, the arrangement of individual and aggregate objectives is a fragile dance. Families, people group, and social orders wrestle with the test of orchestrating dissimilar yearnings into a firm story that cultivates solidarity and progress. The manufacturing of shared objectives in the cauldron of shared values turns into the foundation of cultural turn of events.

Training, as a groundbreaking power, assumes an essential part in forming individual desires and cultural objectives. The most common way of working out instructive goals includes granting information and abilities as well as ingraining a feeling of direction and city obligation. Balanced training furnishes people with the apparatuses to contribute seriously to society and seek after objectives that stretch out past private delight.

The crossing point of innovation and objective setting has introduced another time of conceivable outcomes and difficulties. In the computerized age, data streams endlessly, making a unique setting against which objectives should be formed and sought after. The democratization of data has engaged people to well-spoken and seek after objectives with phenomenal admittance to information and worldwide organizations.

Be that as it may, the pervasiveness of innovation likewise presents a situation with two sides. The constant speed of progress, powered by mechanical headways, requires people and associations to be dexterous and versatile in their objective setting processes. What might be a suitable objective today could be delivered out of date tomorrow by the quick flows of mechanical development.

As the world turns out to be progressively interconnected, the laying out of worldwide objectives has arisen as a basic goal. Difficulties, for example, environmental change, neediness, and pandemics rise above public boundaries, requiring cooperative and coordinated endeavors on a worldwide scale. The working out of worldwide objectives requires a change in perspective from tight personal circumstance to an aggregate ethos that focuses on the prosperity of the planet and its occupants.

The Unified Countries Supportable Improvement Objectives (SDGs) stand as a demonstration of the worldwide local area's acknowledgment of the requirement for shared worldwide targets. These objectives, going from killing destitution to guaranteeing ecological supportability, act as a plan for countries and associations to adjust their endeavors toward normal desires. The most common way of working out worldwide objectives requires conciliatory artfulness, participation, and a common obligation to everyone's benefit.

In the cauldron of business, the fashioning of business objectives is a dynamic and iterative cycle. Business people, as advanced chemists, explore the vulnerabilities of the market to change their dreams into feasible ventures. The working bankrupt objectives implies a fragile harmony between risk-taking and determined independent direction, with the commercial center filling in as the tenacious judge of progress or disappointment.

Besides, the developing idea of work and the idea of a vocation require a consistent course of objective refinement. People explore a vocation scene that is set apart by instability and vulnerability, expecting them to adjust their objectives to evolving monetary, innovative, and cultural circumstances. The conventional direct profession way has given way to a more liquid and nonlinear direction, where people should constantly rethink and recalibrate their objectives.

In the domain of sports, the quest for athletic objectives includes a thorough routine of preparing, discipline, and mental grit. Competitors, as models of objective driven persistence, continually endeavor to push the limits of human potential.

The working out of athletic objectives requires a harmonious connection between actual ability and mental strength, as competitors defy the cauldron of contest and the quest for greatness.

Imaginative undertakings, whether as music, writing, or visual expressions, likewise involve a course of working out innovative objectives. Specialists wrestle with the strain among motivation and discipline, trying to make an interpretation of unique dreams into unmistakable articulations. The fashioning of imaginative objectives includes a persistent exchange between the maker and the medium, with each stroke of the brush or keystroke on the piano filling in as a stage toward understanding the craftsman's vision.

The cultural texture is woven with the strings of aggregate yearnings, and the working out of municipal objectives turns into a common obligation. Administration, as the cauldron of cultural direction, assumes a vital part in molding and carrying out objectives that mirror the necessities and goals of the general population. The most common way of laying out community objectives includes a fragile dance between the voice of individuals and the wise activity of initiative.

Notwithstanding, the adequacy of objective setting in the public area is in many cases dependent upon the straightforwardness of administration and the strength of majority rule foundations. Without a trace of open exchange and comprehensive dynamic cycles, the working out of metro objectives can decay into a hierarchical activity that estranges and disappoints sections of the populace.

The consistently extending boondocks of science and examination likewise request a nuanced way to deal with objective setting. Researchers, as voyagers of the obscure, leave on a persistent journey to grow the limits of human information. The working out of logical objectives includes the quest for explicit disclosures as well as the development of a feeling of interest and request that pushes established researchers forward.

With regards to ecological preservation, the most common way of working out protection objectives is characteristically attached to the sensitive equilibrium of environments. Progressives wrestle with the basic to safeguard biodiversity and regular assets while tending to the necessities of thriving human populaces. The manufacturing of preservation objectives requires an all encompassing methodology that thinks about the reliance of natural frameworks and human prosperity.

The crossing point of morals and objective setting acquaints an ethical aspect with the interaction. The working out of moral objectives includes a scrupulous thought of the effect of one's activities on people, networks, and the more extensive world. Moral contemplations act as the ethical compass that guides people and associations in exploring the mind boggling landscape of direction.

In the domain of medical services, the laying out of clinical objectives includes a pledge to the prosperity of people and networks. Medical services experts, as stewards of human wellbeing, wrestle with the moral objectives of giving consideration, easing enduring, and advancing general wellbeing. The working out of clinical objectives requires a sensitive harmony between the basic to recuperate and the acknowledgment of the moral aspects intrinsic in clinical practice.

The working out of objectives is certainly not a singular undertaking; a collective orchestra reverberates with the music of shared yearnings. Networks, as pots of aggregate character, take part in the powerful course of laying out objectives that mirror their qualities and address their novel difficulties. The fashioning of local area objectives includes a participatory methodology that draws on the insight and experiences of different voices inside the local area.

Besides, the method involved with working out objectives at the local area level requires an acknowledgment of the interconnectedness of nearby and worldwide elements. Networks are not detached elements but rather essential parts of the bigger embroidered artwork of mankind. The manufacturing of local area objectives, subsequently, includes a sensitive transaction between nearby independence and a more extensive consciousness of worldwide interdependencies.

In the pot of relational connections, the putting forth of social objectives turns into a nuanced dance of common comprehension and split the difference. Whether with regards to companionships, heartfelt associations, or familial bonds, people explore the fragile landscape of shared yearnings and individual independence. The working out of social objectives includes open correspondence, compassion, and a common obligation to the development and prosperity of each party included.

The working out of objectives, whether on an individual or aggregate level, is indivisible from the more extensive setting of cultural qualities and standards. Cultural assumptions and social impacts shape the boundaries inside which people well-spoken and seek after their objectives. The pressure between individual independence and cultural assumptions turns into a characterizing component of the objective setting process, expecting people to explore the sensitive harmony between self-articulation and congruity.

In the pot of schooling, the laying out of instructive objectives includes a diverse way to deal with supporting the comprehensive improvement of people. Instructive establishments, as overseers of information and values, assume a significant part in forming the objectives of students. The working out of instructive objectives requires an acknowledgment of the different gifts and goals of understudies, encouraging a climate that develops decisive reasoning, inventiveness, and a feeling of city obligation.

The elements of orientation and objective setting acquaint one more layer of intricacy with the cycle. Orientation standards and cultural assumptions frequently shape the objectives that people, especially ladies, feel engaged to seek after. The working out of orientation comprehensive objectives includes testing generalizations and destroying obstructions that limit people in view of their orientation. A more impartial and comprehensive society is one in which people can well-spoken and seek after objectives regardless of orientation.

With regards to otherworldliness, the working out of profound objectives includes a significant excursion of self-disclosure and association with the extraordinary. People, regardless of strict affiliations, look to develop a feeling of direction and implying that reaches out past the material domain. The fashioning of otherworldly objectives includes reflection, thought, and a journey for existential comprehension that rises above the limits of oneself.

The method involved with working out objectives isn't safe to the recurring pattern of authentic ages. Cultural changes, international movements, and social transformations shape the objectives that people and networks try to accomplish. The working out of objectives in the cauldron of history includes a unique transaction between the climate existing apart from everything else and the persevering through human mission for progress and self-acknowledgment.

4.1 Setting SMART goals for physical fitness

Leaving on an excursion toward actual wellness is an excellent undertaking, and the most common way of laying out objectives turns into an essential move toward this extraordinary journey. The Brilliant rules — Explicit, Quantifiable, Feasible, Pertinent, and Time-Bound — give an organized structure to creating wellness objectives that are rousing as well as helpful for practical advancement.

Particularity lies at the center of successful objective setting for actual wellness. As opposed to setting unclear goals like "getting in shape" or "shedding pounds," it is vital to characterize exactly what you plan to accomplish. For example, a particular objective may be to decrease muscle to fat ratio by a specific sum, increment bulk, or complete a particular number of push-ups. Explicitness improves lucidity, giving a guide to your wellness process and working with centered endeavors.

Quantifiability is the second mainstay of Shrewd objective setting. An objective should be quantifiable, considering substantial following of progress. This includes laying out substantial measurements that empower you to precisely check your headways. Rather than a conventional objective, for example, "further develop perseverance," a quantifiable objective could be to run a specific distance inside a predefined time span or complete a set number of redundancies in strength preparing works out. The capacity to gauge progress cultivates responsibility and gives a feeling of achievement as achievements are reached.

Attainability highlights the significance of putting forth practical objectives that line up with your ongoing wellness level, abilities, and assets. While aspiration is excellent, setting out of reach targets can prompt disappointment and demotivation. Evaluating your beginning stage and logically testing yourself guarantees that objectives are testing yet reachable. For example, in the event that you're new to running, a sensible objective may be to finished a 5K race inside a couple of months, bit by bit expanding the test as your wellness gets to the next level.

Pertinence stresses the arrangement of wellness objectives with your more extensive targets, values, and way of life. An objective that resounds with your own desires is bound to rouse responsibility and determination. Consider how your wellness objectives add to your general prosperity, whether it be upgrading psychological well-being, further developing energy levels, or cultivating a feeling of achievement. An important objective is one that holds characteristic worth and importance with regards to your life.

The fleeting aspect is typified in Time-Bound, underscoring the significance of setting cutoff times for accomplishing your wellness objectives. Laying out a time period makes a need to keep moving and keeps objectives from becoming unassuming goals. As opposed to an obscure objective like "get in shape," a period bound objective may be to lose a particular measure of weight in no less than 90 days or to accomplish a specific degree of adaptability inside a set time period. The consideration of cutoff times works with progress observing and forestalls dawdling.

Applying the Brilliant models to actual wellness objectives requires insightful thought and reflection. Consider a situation where an individual, we should call her Sarah, is setting out on a wellness venture. Applying particularity, Sarah recognizes her objective as diminishing muscle to fat ratio by 5% in six months or less. This particular objective gives a reasonable course to her endeavors.

Quantifiability becomes an integral factor as Sarah chooses to utilize a mix of body estimations and bioelectrical impedance investigation to precisely keep tabs on her development. These quantifiable measurements act as benchmarks, permitting Sarah to commend accomplishments and make informed changes in accordance with her wellness schedule.

As far as feasibility, Sarah surveys her ongoing wellness level, way of life, and accessible assets. Perceiving that a forceful objective could prompt burnout, she changes her objective to line up with a sensible and supportable speed. This guarantees that her wellness process is testing yet feasible, encouraging a feeling of achievement en route.

Importance becomes evident as Sarah thinks about why she needs to decrease muscle versus fat. For her situation, it's about style as well as about advancing by and large wellbeing, upgrading her energy levels, and developing a positive self-perception. The importance of the objective to her more extensive prosperity fortifies her responsibility and inspiration.

To consolidate the time-bound component, Sarah sets a cutoff time of a half year for accomplishing her 5% decrease in muscle versus fat. This time span makes a need to keep moving, provoking Sarah to remain on track and predictable in her endeavors. It additionally permits her to intermittently assess her advancement, change her methodology if necessary, and celebrate achievements en route.

Sarah's situation delineates the groundbreaking force of Brilliant objective setting in the domain of actual wellness. Whether intending to get more fit, form muscle, work on cardiovascular wellbeing, or upgrade adaptability, the Shrewd rules act as a flexible device for molding goals that are both persuading and feasible.

Chasing actual wellness, objective setting is certainly not a one-time occasion yet an iterative interaction that develops with evolving conditions, encounters, and goals. As people progress on their wellness process, the refinement and recalibration of objectives become vital to supported development and long haul prosperity.

The foundation of present moment and long haul objectives makes a guide for steady advancement. Momentary objectives, feasible inside half a month or months, give quick focuses on that add to the satisfaction of more extensive, long haul targets. For example, a transient objective could be to expand the quantity of week after week exercises or to integrate more vegetables into day to day dinners. These more modest achievements add to the general direction of the wellness venture.

Long haul objectives, then again, mirror the all-encompassing yearnings
that people have for their actual wellness. These objectives might traverse a while or even years and frequently act as the core values that shape the heading of one's wellness process. Instances of long haul objectives could incorporate accomplishing and keeping a particular body weight, finishing a long distance race, or dominating high level yoga presents. Long haul objectives give a feeling of motivation and bearing, mooring the wellness venture in a more extensive setting.

The idea of moderate over-burden is a crucial guideline in wellness objective setting. It includes slowly expanding the force, length, or intricacy of exercises to animate continuous enhancements in strength, perseverance, and generally speaking wellness. Moderate over-burden guarantees that the body is persistently tested, forestalling levels and advancing supported progress. Wellness objectives, accordingly, ought to be dynamic, considering intermittent acclimations to oblige the guideline of moderate over-burden.

Versatility is a significant part of successful objective setting in the domain of actual wellness. Life is intrinsically unique, and unanticipated conditions might influence one's capacity to stick to a predefined plan.

An adaptable way to deal with objective setting permits people to adjust their targets in view of evolving needs, timetables, or wellbeing contemplations. This flexibility encourages versatility and keeps difficulties from crashing the general wellness venture.

The significance of objective arrangement with individual inclinations and interests couldn't possibly be more significant. Pleasure and satisfaction in proactive tasks contribute fundamentally to objective adherence and long haul supportability. Picking exercises that resound with individual inclinations, whether it be running, cycling, weightlifting, or gathering wellness classes, improves inspiration and makes the wellness venture more charming. Adjusting objectives to exercises that carry fulfillment encourages a positive relationship with work out.

Social help assumes an essential part in the accomplishment of wellness objectives. Offering objectives to companions, family, or exercise accomplices makes an emotionally supportive network that gives consolation, responsibility, and kinship. The aggregate quest for wellness objectives encourages a feeling of local area, making the excursion more pleasant and building up responsibility during testing times. Social help can take different structures, including exercise amigos, bunch classes, or virtual networks that share comparable wellness desires.

Observing and following advancement are fundamental parts of effective objective achievement. Normal evaluations, like wellness appraisals, body estimations, or execution benchmarks, give objective information that mirror the effect of one's endeavors. Following advancement not just approves the viability of the picked approach yet additionally fills in as a wellspring of inspiration, as people observer unmistakable enhancements over the long run. Celebrating little triumphs en route supports a positive mentality and reinforces certainty.

Integrating assortment into the wellness routine isn't just a methodology for forestalling tedium yet additionally a method for tending to various parts of actual wellness. A balanced methodology that incorporates cardiovascular activity, strength preparing, adaptability work, and useful developments guarantees thorough wellness improvement. Broadening the kinds of exercises participated in adds to in general wellbeing, diminishes the gamble of abuse wounds, and keeps the wellness venture drawing in and dynamic.

Dietary contemplations are essential to the accomplishment of actual wellness objectives. The saying "you can't out-practice a terrible eating routine" highlights the meaning of dietary decisions related to active work. Adjusting nourishing objectives, like consuming a fair eating routine, remaining hydrated, and overseeing segment sizes, with in general wellness goals upgrades the viability of the wellness venture. Sustenance is a critical part in supporting energy levels, recuperation, and the body's capacity to adjust to the requests of activity.

4.2 Creating a personalized workout and nutrition plan

Setting out on an excursion to work on one's wellness and by and large prosperity is an excellent undertaking. Vital to this pursuit is the formation of a customized exercise and nourishment plan, a dynamic and individualized guide that incorporates actual work and dietary decisions. Creating such an arrangement includes smart thought of individual objectives, wellness levels, inclinations, and way of life factors.

The Establishment: Objective Setting

At the core of making a customized exercise and sustenance plan is the foundation of clear and reasonable objectives. These objectives act as the directing power that shapes the parts of the arrangement, giving a feeling of motivation and heading. Whether the targets are based on weight reduction, muscle gain, worked on cardiovascular wellbeing, or improved generally wellness, articulating explicit and quantifiable objectives is the underlying step.

The Shrewd standards — Explicit, Quantifiable, Reachable, Important, and Time-Bound — offer an organized system for objective setting. Particularity guarantees that objectives are obviously characterized, ruling out equivocalness. Quantifiability takes into consideration objective following of headway, empowering people to praise accomplishments and make informed changes. Attainability accentuates defining reasonable objectives that line up with one's capacities and assets. Pertinence highlights the significance of adjusting objectives to more extensive yearnings and values. Time-Bound includes laying out cutoff times, cultivating a need to get going and responsibility.

For instance, a particular and quantifiable objective could be to shed 10 pounds in the span of 90 days through a mix of activity and nourishment. This objective is reachable by setting a reasonable objective in light of individual factors like current weight, digestion, and way of life. The pertinence of the objective could be attached to generally wellbeing improvement and expanded energy levels. Ultimately, the time-bound component lays out a need to keep moving, empowering predictable endeavors over the assigned period.

Creating the Exercise Plan: Assortment and Movement

A customized exercise plan ought to be custom-made to individual inclinations, wellness levels, and way of life imperatives. The incorporation of assortment forestalls tedium as well as addresses various features of actual wellness. A balanced methodology commonly consolidates cardiovascular activities, strength preparing, adaptability work, and utilitarian developments.

Cardiovascular activities, like running, cycling, or swimming, add to heart wellbeing and calorie use. Strength preparing, including opposition practices like weightlifting, constructs bulk, helps digestion, and improves by and large strength.

Adaptability work, through exercises like yoga or extending schedules, advances joint versatility and decreases the gamble of wounds. Useful developments emulate exercises of day to day living, cultivating further developed equilibrium, coordination, and solid perseverance.

Moderate over-burden, a basic rule in wellness, includes progressively expanding the force, span, or intricacy of exercises to animate continuous upgrades. This guideline guarantees that the body is reliably tested, forestalling levels and advancing supported progress. A very much organized exercise plan consolidates moderate over-burden in a calculated manner, considering the variation of the body to shifting degrees of stress.

The recurrence and span of exercises rely upon individual factors like wellness objectives, time accessibility, and recuperation limit. For example, a fledgling could begin with three to four meetings each week, steadily advancing as wellness levels get to the next level. The power of exercises can be regulated by changing variables like loads, redundancies, or running pace.

Remembering both opposition and vigorous activities for the plan is fundamental. Obstruction preparing constructs fit bulk, which, thus, supports digestion and adds to long haul weight the board. Cardiovascular activities improve heart wellbeing, consume calories, and add to generally speaking wellness. The mix of these components makes a balanced and successful gym routine everyday practice.

Individualization and Flexibility

Personalization is a critical part of an effective exercise plan. Fitting activities to individual inclinations and tending to explicit necessities or impediments cultivates commitment and adherence. For somebody who appreciates outside exercises, consolidating running in a close by park or cycling on tourist detours could improve the happiness regarding the exercise. On the other hand, people who favor the construction of a rec center climate could find strength preparing with loads seriously engaging.

Flexibility is one more urgent component of a customized exercise plan. Life is intrinsically unique, and unexpected conditions might influence one's capacity to stick to a predefined work-out daily schedule. An adaptable methodology permits people to adjust their exercise plan in light of evolving needs, timetables, or wellbeing contemplations. This versatility cultivates flexibility and keeps mishaps from wrecking the general wellness venture.

The Job of Sustenance: Energizing the Body

Supplementing the exercise plan, a powerful nourishment system is fundamental for accomplishing wellness objectives. Nourishment gives the fuel that powers exercises, upholds recuperation, and impacts body sythesis. Creating a customized sustenance plan includes an equilibrium of macronutrients (sugars, proteins, and fats), micronutrients (nutrients and minerals), and hydration.

Understanding individual caloric requirements is an essential move toward healthful preparation. The quantity of calories required is impacted by elements, for example, basal metabolic rate, actual work level, and objectives (weight reduction, support, or muscle gain). Online number crunchers or counsel with a nutritionist can assist with deciding a fitting caloric objective.

Macronutrients assume particular parts in the body, and their conveyance ought to line up with individual objectives. Sugars are an essential energy source, especially significant for filling extraordinary exercises. Proteins support muscle fix and development, making them essential for those planning to construct or keep up with fit bulk. Fats add to by and large wellbeing and are fundamental for the assimilation of fat-solvent nutrients.

A fair and changed diet that incorporates a range of beautiful organic products, vegetables, lean proteins, entire grains, and solid fats guarantees an expansive exhibit of supplements. The idea of supplement timing — decisively consuming supplements previously, during, and after exercises — improves execution and recuperation. For instance, having a blend of starches and proteins post-exercise helps muscle glycogen renewal and fix.

Hydration is frequently misjudged yet is fundamental to generally wellbeing and exercise execution. Lack of hydration can weaken physical and mental capability, prevent recuperation, and effect perseverance. Sufficient water consumption, custom fitted to individual requirements and action levels, upholds ideal hydration.

Careful Eating and Part Control

Past macronutrients and hydration, careful eating and piece control contribute essentially to the viability of a nourishment plan. Careful eating includes focusing on hunger signs, enjoying flavors, and perceiving totality. It beats close to home or diverted eating down, advancing a better relationship with food.

Segment control is a commonsense methodology to oversee caloric admission. While the nature of food decisions is foremost, segment sizes impact by and large energy balance. Procedures like utilizing more modest plates, monitoring serving sizes, and keeping away from careless eating can add to partition control.

Individualized Contemplations: Medical issue and Inclinations

Individual medical issue and dietary inclinations assume a vital part in forming both exercise and nourishment plans. For people with previous ailments, talking with medical services experts or enlisted dietitians guarantees that activity and nourishment methodologies line up with clinical proposals.

Dietary inclinations, like vegetarianism or veganism, can be obliged by creating nourishment designs that meet explicit wholesome necessities while lining up with moral or way of life decisions. Adaptability and imagination in feast arranging add to the manageability of dietary inclinations.

For those with explicit wellness goals, like preparation for a long distance race or planning for a strength rivalry, specific exercise plans custom-made to the requests of the occasion become fundamental. These plans frequently include periodization, an organized methodology that partitions preparing into particular stages, each zeroing in on unambiguous wellness credits.

Checking and Changing the Arrangement

Predictable checking and occasional reassessment are basic parts of both exercise and sustenance plans. Normal appraisals, like wellness assessments, body estimations, or execution benchmarks, give objective information that mirror the effect of endeavors. Observing advancement not just approves the viability of the picked approach yet additionally fills in as a wellspring of inspiration.

Changing the arrangement in light of criticism from observing guarantees that it stays lined up with developing objectives and conditions. For example, in the event that weight reduction slows down, acclimations to caloric admission or exercise power might be fundamental. In the event that strength acquires level, altering the opposition preparing system can revitalize progress.

Social Help and Responsibility

The incorporation of social help improves the viability of customized exercise and nourishment plans. Offering objectives to companions, family, or exercise accomplices makes an emotionally supportive network that gives consolation, responsibility, and kinship. The aggregate quest for wellness objectives cultivates a feeling of local area, making the excursion more charming and supporting responsibility during testing times.

4.3 Tracking progress and making adjustments along the way

Leaving on an excursion towards self-awareness, whether it be in wellness, profession, or some other part of life, requires a promise to persistent improvement. Following headway and making changes en route is a significant part of this extraordinary interaction. This powerful methodology guarantees that objectives stay pertinent, practical, and versatile to the consistently changing conditions of life.

The Meaning of Progress Following

Powerful advancement following fills in as a compass, giving bits of knowledge into the viability of procedures and the arrangement of endeavors with wanted results. It offers a substantial and objective proportion of progression, encouraging inspiration and a feeling of achievement. Also, progress following works with informed navigation, empowering people to make acclimations to their arrangements in view of genuine information as opposed to suspicions or instinct.

In the domain of actual wellness, following advancement takes on different structures, going from basic measurements like weight and body estimations to additional perplexing pointers, for example, strength levels, perseverance, and adaptability.

Normal evaluations offer a thorough preview of the effect of way of life changes, giving a premise to refining gym routine schedules and wholesome procedures.

The Measurements of Wellness Progress

Body Weight and Piece: While weight alone doesn't give a total image of wellness, it tends to be a valuable metric when thought about close by different elements. Changes in body piece, for example, a decrease in muscle to fat ratio or an expansion in fit bulk, are more demonstrative of progress than simple variances in weight.

Estimations: Following circumferential estimations of key regions, like abdomen, hips, chest, arms, and legs, offers experiences into changes in body shape. Progress in these estimations might demonstrate fat misfortune, muscle gain, or upgrades in generally conditioning and definition.

Strength Levels: Strength is a crucial part of wellness, and enhancements in strength levels are many times substantial markers of progress. Following the loads lifted in obstruction preparing works out, the quantity of redundancies performed, or the capacity to lift heavier burdens over the long haul gives a quantitative proportion of solidarity gains.

Perseverance and Cardiovascular Wellness: For those zeroing in on cardiovascular wellbeing, following perseverance markers like running distance, cycling length, or swimming laps can be significant. Upgrades in these measurements recommend improved cardiovascular wellness and endurance.

Adaptability and Scope of Movement: Adaptability is a critical part of in general wellness and frequently ignored. Consistently surveying adaptability through practices like extending schedules or yoga presents permits people to screen enhancements in scope of movement and joint adaptability.

Execution Measurements: Contingent upon explicit wellness objectives, execution measurements connected with specific exercises can act as important markers. This could incorporate running times, the quantity of push-ups or pull-ups performed, or accomplishments in unambiguous wellness challenges.

Nourishing Advancement Following

Caloric Admission and Macronutrients: Observing everyday caloric admission and the conveyance of macronutrients (carbs, proteins, and fats) gives bits of knowledge into dietary propensities. Understanding how nourishing decisions line up with individual objectives — whether it be weight reduction, muscle gain, or in general prosperity — empowers changes for ideal results.

Food Journaling: Keeping a food diary gives a subjective record of dietary decisions. This training energizes care and mindfulness, featuring designs, triggers for undesirable eating, and potential open doors for development.

Hydration: Satisfactory hydration is frequently misjudged yet assumes a critical part in generally wellbeing and prosperity. Following everyday water consumption guarantees that the body remains enough hydrated, supporting ideal physiological capabilities.

Dinner Timing: The planning of feasts and tidbits can affect energy levels, absorption, and generally supplement use. Following feast timing gives experiences into eating designs and can be changed in accordance with enhance execution and prosperity.

Supplement Thickness: Zeroing in on the supplement thickness of food varieties — picking those plentiful in nutrients, minerals, and other fundamental supplements — adds to by and large wellbeing. Following supplement thick decisions guarantees a reasonable and differed diet.

Mental and Way of life Measurements

State of mind and Energy Levels: Mental prosperity is entwined with actual wellbeing. Observing temperament and energy levels offers a subjective evaluation of how way of life decisions, including activity and sustenance, influence in general mental and profound states.

Rest Quality and Term: Quality rest is fundamental for recuperation, execution, and generally speaking wellbeing. Following rest designs, including term and quality, gives bits of knowledge into the adequacy of rest cleanliness rehearses.

Feelings of anxiety: Persistent pressure can impede progress in different parts of life, including wellness. Following feelings of anxiety, recognizing triggers, and executing pressure the board techniques add to a comprehensive way to deal with prosperity.

Consistency: Consistency is a critical calculate long haul achievement. Following the consistency of gym routine schedules, adherence to nourishing plans, and way of life propensities offers a proportion of devotion and responsibility.

The Iterative Course of Changes

The excursion towards self-awareness and accomplishment is seldom a straight way. Life is dynamic, introducing difficulties, valuable open doors, and unforeseen turns. Making changes en route is certainly not an indication of disappointment however a demonstration of flexibility, versatility, and a guarantee to ceaseless improvement.

Reflection and Assessment:

Ordinary reflection and assessment of progress are fundamental parts of the change cycle. This includes returning to beginning objectives, looking at them against current status, and surveying what has and hasn't worked. Intelligent practices, for example, journaling or self-evaluation, give an organized way to deal with thoughtfulness.

Information Driven Direction:

Information, whether quantitative or subjective, structures the reason for informed direction. Examining progress following measurements impartially permits people to recognize examples, patterns, and regions for development. This information driven approach guarantees that changes depend on proof instead of abstract discernments.

Perceiving Levels and Difficulties:

Levels and difficulties are normal events in any excursion of self-improvement. Perceiving when progress slows down or makes a stride back is a significant piece of the change cycle. Rather than review mishaps as disappointments, they ought to be viewed as any open doors for learning and refining systems.

Changes in accordance with Exercise Plans:

Power and Volume: Moderate over-burden, the progressive expansion in the force or volume of exercises, is a basic guideline in wellness. Assuming advancement slows down, changing the power or volume of exercises — whether by expanding loads, changing work-out schedules, or integrating new exercises — invigorates the body to adjust and develop.

Assortment and Broadly educating: Bringing assortment into gym routine schedules forestalls fatigue as well as difficulties different muscle gatherings and energy frameworks. Broadly educating, consolidating different exercises like swimming, cycling, or yoga, offers a break from routine while adding to by and large wellness.

Rest and Recuperation: Overtraining can impede progress and increment the gamble of wounds. Changing the recurrence and power of exercises to consider sufficient rest and recuperation is critical. Integrating rest days into the week by week schedule and focusing on rest are fundamental parts of a compelling change procedure.

Periodization: Periodization includes arranging preparing into particular stages, each with explicit targets. Changing exercise plans through periodization considers designated center around various parts of wellness, forestalling levels and enhancing generally speaking execution.

Changes in accordance with Sustenance Plans:

Caloric Admission: In the event that weight reduction or muscle gain slows down, changing caloric admission is a typical system.

This change can include a slight decrease in calories for weight reduction or a humble increment for muscle gain. Offsetting caloric admission with consumption guarantees an energy balance helpful for objectives.

Macronutrient Proportions: The dissemination of macronutrients in the eating routine impacts body piece and execution. Changing macronutrient proportions —, for example, expanding protein admission for muscle gain or changing starch levels for perseverance competitors — adjusts healthful decisions to explicit targets.

Supplement Timing: Tweaking supplement timing can improve execution and recuperation. Changing pre-and post-exercise nourishment, as well as feast timing over the course of the day, guarantees that the body gets the vital fuel at key times.

Hydration Systems: Changing hydration procedures in light of movement levels, environment, and individual requirements is critical. Expanded actual work or sweltering weather conditions might require higher liquid admission. Observing pee tone and focusing on thirst prompts are commonsense ways of evaluating hydration status.

Mental Changes:

Outlook and Inspiration: Mental prosperity impacts actual results. Changing mentality and inspiration includes reconsidering objectives, distinguishing inherent inspirations, and developing a positive and versatile viewpoint. Procedures like representation, positive certifications, and objective reassessment add to mental changes.

Stress The executives: Stress, whenever left unmanaged, can block progress. Changing pressure the board systems, whether through contemplation, profound breathing activities, or taking part in loosening up exercises, upholds in general prosperity.

Systems for Defeating Misfortunes:

Learning Amazing open doors: Mishaps, whether in wellness or different everyday issues, offer important learning potential open doors. Rather than review misfortunes as unfavorable impediments, move toward them with a development outlook. Break down the elements adding to mishaps, distinguish illustrations learned, and utilize this information to refine future methodologies.

Versatile Objective Setting: Assuming that underlying objectives demonstrate testing or ridiculous, consider changing them to more readily line up with current conditions. Versatile objective laying out includes perceiving when objectives need adjustment and setting new focuses on that are testing yet feasible.

Social Help: During testing times, looking for help from companions, family, or a local area with comparative objectives can give support and responsibility. Imparting misfortunes to others encourages a feeling of aggregate comprehension and shared obligation to defeating difficulties.

Proficient Direction: Looking for direction from wellness experts, nutritionists, or emotional well-being specialists can give significant experiences. Experts can offer customized exhortation, recognize regions for development, and guide the change cycle with ability.

The Consistent Pattern of Progress Following and Changes:
Progress following and changes structure a nonstop cycle instead of a one-time occasion. As people develop and advance, so do their objectives, conditions, and needs. The iterative course of evaluating progress, making changes, and putting forth new objectives guarantees that self-improvement stays dynamic and versatile.

Long haul Maintainability and Way of life Coordination:
A definitive point of progress following and changes is to add to long haul maintainability and way of life coordination. Wellness and self-awareness are not transient undertakings but rather long lasting excursions. Reasonable propensities and practices flawlessly coordinated into day to day existence become inherent parts of a solid and satisfying way of life.

Chapter 5

The Furnace of Resilience

In the cauldron of misfortune, human strength is manufactured. A quality rises above difficulty, a demonstration of the unyielding soul inside every person. The heater of flexibility shines brilliantly despite difficulties, refining character and forming predeterminations. This excursion through the cauldron is generally difficult, however it is in these searing preliminaries that we find the genuine proportion of our solidarity.

Life, with all its unconventionality, is a determined educator. It tosses curves unexpectedly, testing the guts of the people who explore its turbulent waters. The heater of flexibility is stirred up by the flames of difficulty, requesting that people rise like a phoenix after their hardships more grounded and stronger than any time in recent memory.

One such story of strength starts in the peaceful rural areas of a modest community, where a young lady named Emily ends up push into the pot of life sooner than she might have envisioned. Brought up in a sustaining climate, Emily had forever been safeguarded from the unforgiving real factors that looked for her in the rest of the world. Much to her dismay that the heater of versatility would before long turn into her pot.

At the age of 22, Emily confronted an unforeseen misfortune that broke the charming air pocket of her reality. The unexpected loss of her folks in an unfortunate mishap left her dispossessed and uncontrolled in an ocean of sadness. The world she once knew disintegrated around her, and the glow of her experience growing up home turned cold and void. It was in this murkiness that Emily found the main flashes of her flexibility.

The underlying shock and sorrow took steps to consume her, however Emily, as liquid metal, started to come to fruition in the cauldron of her aggravation. She drew strength from the recollections of her folks, involving their adoration as a directing light through the haziest days. The heater of strength consumed inside her, producing an assurance to reconstruct her life from the remains of misery.

Emily's process was set apart by mishaps and snags, yet with every preliminary, her versatility developed further. She confronted monetary battles, exploring the intricacies of adulthood without the direction of her folks. The heater inside her copied more splendid, filling a tireless quest for self-disclosure and strengthening.

As Emily wandered into the labor force, she experienced difficulties that tried her expert abilities as well as her flexibility despite difficulty. The serious idea of her picked profession way requested relentlessness and coarseness, characteristics that Emily had developed in the heater of her own battles. Dismissals and difficulties became venturing stones, and every disappointment energized her assurance to transcend the conditions.

The pot of flexibility isn't restricted to individual stories; it reaches out to the aggregate human experience. Social orders, as well, face their preliminaries, and the heater of strength consumes inside networks endeavoring to beat shared difficulties. History is packed with instances of countries miraculously rising like a phoenix after war, financial slumps, and cataclysmic events, their flexibility an encouraging sign for people in the future.

Consider the strength of a country recuperating from the repercussions of a staggering struggle. The scars of war run profound, leaving networks cracked and economies in ruins. However, in the cauldron of post-war reproduction, versatility turns into the impetus for restoration. Individuals meet up, modifying actual designs as well as the social texture that ties them. The heater of versatility changes the aggregate injury into a power for positive change, fashioning a way towards a more promising time to come.

The strength of countries is in many cases tried by catastrophic events, where the powers of nature release their rage with little respect for human lines. In the consequence of tremors, tropical storms, or waves, networks wind up wrestling with misfortune and obliteration. However, it is at these times of emergency that the heater of flexibility blasts, manufacturing obligations of fortitude and moving demonstrations of empathy.

Consider a seaside town desolated by a wave, where homes are decreased to rubble, and the once-flourishing local area is diminished to flotsam and jetsam. Notwithstanding such annihilation, the heater of flexibility thunders to life. Neighbors become mainstays of help, outsiders loan some assistance, and the local area mobilizes together to reconstruct what was lost. The versatility that rises out of the destruction turns into the establishment for a more grounded, all the more closely knit society.

The worldwide local area, as well, isn't resistant to the preliminaries that test the heater of flexibility. Issues, for example, environmental change, pandemics, and financial emergencies require an aggregate reaction that draws on the strength of countries and people the same. The difficulties might be overwhelming, however the human limit with regards to versatility is unlimited.

Think about the world's reaction to a worldwide pandemic, where the undetectable danger of a viral flare-up pushes countries to the brink of collapse. The heater of strength is lighted as medical services experts work indefatigably on the bleeding edges, researchers attempt to beat the clock to foster immunizations, and networks adjust to better approaches for living. In the cauldron of a pandemic, the versatility of humankind is on full showcase, as individuals meet up to safeguard the defenseless, support neighborhood organizations, and track down creative answers for uncommon difficulties.

The heater of strength is definitely not a one-time cauldron; it is a dependable friend in the excursion of life. As people and social orders explore the always changing scenes of presence, they are over and over push into the flames of affliction. It is at these times that the genuine strength of flexibility is uncovered, as individuals come back to life, reawakened and reestablished.

The excursion of flexibility isn't without its oddities. It is in weakness that strength is found, in give up that strengthening flourishes. The heater of versatility isn't tied in with opposing the intensity yet embracing it, permitting the blazes to shape and form people into creatures of courage and effortlessness. It is a hit the dance floor with the fire, a tango of give up and obstruction that characterizes the substance of strength.

In the pot of flexibility, there is a significant insight that arises. The comprehension life's difficulties are not snags to be kept away from yet amazing open doors for development. The heater of strength instructs that disappointment isn't a loss yet a venturing stone to progress, that aggravation isn't a foe yet an educator, and that difficulty isn't a revile however an impetus for change.

The excursion through the heater of flexibility is profoundly private, a lone journey through the profundities of one's spirit. It is a journey for self-revelation, a persistent quest for the genuine self that rises up out of the pot of preliminaries. The flexibility that is brought into the world at these times isn't an exterior however a center strength that endures everyday hardship.

As people explore the maze of their own cauldrons, they frequently end up wrestling with existential inquiries. What is the motivation behind the anguish? For what reason must one get through the flames of misfortune? In the journey for significance, the heater of flexibility turns into a pot of thoughtfulness, where people stand up to their most profound feelings of dread and disentangle the secrets of their reality.

The existential excursion through the heater of strength isn't for weak willed. It requires an eagerness to defy the shadows inside, to embrace the distress of vulnerability, and to give up to the groundbreaking force of weakness. It is an excursion of drop and climb, a repeating hit the dance floor with the self that reflects the timeless back and forth movement of life.

In the pot of flexibility, people frequently find a significant association with an option that could be more significant than themselves. Whether it be a feeling of direction, a profound arousing, or a recharged obligation to a reason, the heater of flexibility opens entryways to greatness. Amidst torment, people see as significance, and in the cinders of sadness, they uncover the seeds of a more significant and genuine presence.

The heater of versatility is certainly not a singular excursion; a common odyssey ties people together in an embroidery of aggregate strength. Networks that weather conditions storms, countries that come back to life, and a worldwide society that faces shared difficulties — all draw from a similar wellspring of flexibility. It is a demonstration of the interconnectedness of the human experience, where the flares of one individual's versatility enlighten the way for other people.

The excursion through the heater of flexibility is set apart by snapshots of significant change. It is in these cauldrons that people shed the layers of molding and cultural assumptions, arising as real creatures unburdened by the heaviness of outer approval. The strength that arises isn't a presentation for a group of people however a real articulation of oneself.

In the pot of versatility, people additionally stand up to the mystery of control and give up. The heater instructs that there are parts of life unchangeable as far as one might be concerned, that the flames of affliction can't be stifled all of the time. However, in the acquiescence to what can't be changed, people find the ability to shape their reaction, to pick strength notwithstanding the wild.

The excursion through the heater of flexibility isn't straight; a twisting circles back on itself, returning to subjects and difficulties in new and developing ways. Every upheaval brings further bits of knowledge, more noteworthy insight, and a more refined comprehension of oneself. The heater of strength turns into a buddy in the continuous course of development and advancement.

As people explore the exciting bends in the road of their own pots, they frequently find comfort in the narratives of other people who have strolled comparable ways. The aggregate insight of the people who have confronted difficulty turns into a directing light, offering bits of knowledge and examples that rise above the singular excursion. In the common accounts of versatility, people find reverberations of their own battles and wins.

The heater of flexibility likewise has a generational aspect. Guardians pass down the blazes of flexibility to their kids, imparting in them the solidarity to confront life's difficulties. The interchange of generational versatility makes a heritage that rises above individual lifetimes, winding around an embroidery of solidarity and strength that traverses across the ages.

In the pot of versatility, there is a call to embrace the full range of human experience. It is an encouragement to hit the dance floor with delight in snapshots of win and to lament completely in the midst of misfortune. The heater instructs that versatility isn't the shortfall of agony yet the ability to hold it, to change enduring into a wellspring of intelligence and sympathy.

The excursion through the heater of strength is likewise a call to develop self-sympathy. Notwithstanding disappointment, mishaps, and snapshots of weakness, people should figure out how to stretch out the very graciousness to themselves that they would propose to a dear companion. The heater of versatility consumes most brilliant when filled by the glow of self esteem and acknowledgment.

As people navigate the cauldron of strength, they frequently find that the excursion isn't tied in with arriving at a last objective yet about embracing the continuous course of becoming. The heater instructs that flexibility is definitely not a static state yet a unique power that develops with each new test. It is a guarantee to development, a readiness to adjust, and an acknowledgment that the actual excursion is the objective.

In the excellent embroidery of the human experience, the heater of flexibility winds around a story of win over misfortune, of development through battle, and of the unyielding soul that beats all chances. It is a story written in the quiet language of the heart, where the blazes of flexibility consume as a demonstration of the human limit with regards to mental fortitude, strength, and elegance.

The heater of versatility calls people to embrace the difficulties that lie ahead, to hit the dance floor with the flares of difficulty, and to rise up out of the pot more grounded, smarter, and stronger than at any other time. A timeless fire enlightens the way of the human excursion, an encouraging sign that rises above the obscurity and guides people towards the brilliant sunrise of their most genuine selves.

In the pot of flexibility, people find that they are not characterized by their conditions but rather by their reaction to them. The heater consumes with extreme heat the deceptions of feebleness, uncovering the inborn strength that dwells inside. A disclosure engages people to recover organization over their lives, to shape their fates with the very hands that once shuddered despite misfortune.

As the excursion through the heater of strength unfurls, people observe that they are in good company. The blazes that manufacture their solidarity are shared by innumerable other people who have confronted comparable preliminaries. In the aggregate dance of versatility, a feeling of having a place arises — an acknowledgment that the human soul is interconnected, strong, and equipped for facing the hardships of life.

The heater of strength is a demonstration of the excellence that rises out of the cauldron of difficulty. It is notwithstanding difficulties that people find the full range of their mankind — their ability for adoration, sympathy, and strength. The flares that once taken steps to consume become the speculative chemistry of change, transforming torment into astuteness, distress into sympathy, and gloom into trust.

In the cauldron of flexibility, people discover that the excursion isn't about flawlessness however about realness. It is a call to embrace the chaotic, defective excellence of the human experience and to perceive that weakness isn't a shortcoming yet a wellspring of solidarity. The heater instructs that versatility isn't tied in with being solid however about being flexible, bowing without breaking, and arising more grounded for the excursion.

The excursion through the heater of strength is a holy journey — a spirit's odyssey through the flames of change. An excursion rises above reality, winding around a story that reverberations through the ages. In the quiet passageways of the human heart, the blazes of versatility gleam as an update that, regardless of how challenging the way, the human soul has the ability to rise, reawakened and brilliant, from the cinders of difficulty.

5.1 Resilience as a key factor in overcoming setbacks

Versatility, the ability to return from difficulty, remains as a foundation of human strength. The backbone pushes people forward when confronted with difficulties, difficulties, and life's unavoidable curves. The excursion through mishaps is widespread, rising above social, cultural, and individual limits. In investigating flexibility as a vital calculate beating difficulties, we dive into the unpredictable snare of human experience, where the seeds of solidarity are in many cases planted in the dirt of difficulty.

Misfortunes come in different structures — a bombed project, the conclusion of a friendship, a wellbeing emergency, or the passing of a task. No matter what the idea of the mishap, the human reaction to misfortune is a demonstration of the inborn limit with regards to versatility.

It is even with mishaps that people find the profundity of their inward supplies, taking advantage of a wellspring of solidarity that might have stayed torpid in less testing times.

Consider the narrative of Sarah, a youthful business person whose undertaking confronted an unexpected slump. The mishap was not simply monetary; it shook the groundworks of her personality and reason. In the cauldron of difficulty, strength arose as a directing power. Sarah explored the consequence with a mix of coarseness and versatility, reconsidering her business methodology, looking for mentorship, and utilizing the misfortune as a chance for development. The experience changed her underlying disappointment into a venturing stone for future achievement.

Versatility is certainly not a static quality; it is a unique interaction formed by one's reaction to misfortune. Clinicians frequently recognize individual flexibility and logical versatility — the capacity to quickly return from individual difficulties and the limit of networks or associations to endure and recuperate from difficulties. The two types of flexibility are interconnected, mirroring the cooperative connection between individual strength and the strong organizations that encompass them.

Individual flexibility is a multi-layered develop, impacted by variables like disposition, survival techniques, and outlook. A few people show a characteristic strength, apparently resolute by mishaps, while others foster versatility through life encounters. The interchange among hereditary qualities and climate adds to the mind boggling embroidery of individual versatility, with both nature and sustain assuming vital parts.

Sarah's story represents the job of outlook in encouraging flexibility. Her capacity to see the mishap as a chance for learning and development represents a development outlook — a conviction that difficulties are venturing stones to progress instead of outlandish snags. Developing a development outlook includes reexamining difficulties as significant encounters, embracing the inconvenience of disappointment, and survey exertion as a way to dominance. In the cauldron of difficulties, a development mentality turns into an impetus for flexibility, changing difficulties into valuable open doors for individual and expert turn of events.

Past individual versatility, the aggregate strength of networks and associations assumes a critical part in conquering mishaps. A people group's capacity to weather conditions difficulties is impacted by variables like social union, shared values, and a feeling of aggregate viability — the conviction that the local area can team up successfully to accomplish shared objectives. In the consequence of difficulties, networks frequently rally together, drawing strength from their common bonds and versatility as an aggregate power.

Associations, as well, explore misfortunes from the perspective of flexibility. The capacity to adjust to evolving conditions, gain from disappointments, and cultivate a culture of development are vital parts of hierarchical versatility.

In a quickly developing world, organizations and foundations that focus on versatility as an essential resource position themselves to endure misfortunes as well as flourish even with vulnerability.

The idea of strength stretches out past brain science and hierarchical hypothesis — it saturates different fields, from nature to designing. In the normal world, environments show strength notwithstanding aggravations, adjusting and recovering to keep up with their capabilities. Engineers plan tough frameworks fit for enduring unforeseen shocks, encapsulating the rule that difficulties are an intrinsic piece of any mind boggling framework's life cycle.

In the domain of human connections, versatility is a foundation of close to home prosperity. The bonds manufactured in the cauldron of misfortunes frequently develop, making a repository of trust and backing. Consider the experience of a couple confronting a relationship emergency. In exploring the difficulties, their flexibility as people and as a unit turns into a groundbreaking power. The capacity to convey straightforwardly, feel for one another's points of view, and adjust to changing elements encourages versatility inside the relationship.

Strength isn't inseparable from resistance; rather, it is the ability to explore weakness with fortitude and versatility. The affirmation of agony, disillusionment, and sadness is a vital piece of the strength venture. People who embrace weakness, permitting themselves to feel and handle the feelings related with difficulties, frequently arise more grounded on the opposite side. It is an incomprehensible dance — a sensitive interaction between recognizing weakness and bringing the solidarity to persist.

The field of positive brain science has contributed altogether to the comprehension of flexibility, accentuating the significance of encouraging positive feelings, qualities, and excellencies in exploring life's difficulties. Versatility, according to this viewpoint, isn't just a receptive reaction to misfortunes yet a functioning development of mental prosperity. Practices like appreciation, care, and cultivating positive connections add to the improvement of a strong outlook, giving people a powerful establishment to confront difficulty.

The account of versatility unfurls in the tales of people who have confronted difficulties and arisen more grounded. Take the case of James, a competitor whose promising vocation was wrecked by a profession undermining injury. The misfortune might have denoted the finish of his athletic excursion, however flexibility impelled him to reclassify his character and reason. James embraced recovery sincerely, turning towards instructing and mentorship. In the pot of difficulty, his flexibility changed a misfortune into another part of satisfaction and commitment.

The job of social help in building flexibility couldn't possibly be more significant. People are innately friendly creatures, and the strength got from strong connections turns into a support point in the flexibility venture.

Companions, family, coaches, and networks give a wellbeing net — an aggregate hug that supports people when mishaps take steps to maneuver them into the pit of depression. The capacity to share one's weaknesses and look for help cultivates a feeling of association, relieving the disconnecting effect of mishaps.

Flexibility is certainly not a lone undertaking; a common excursion meshes the strings of individual strength into the texture of networks. In the midst of emergency, the aggregate flexibility of a local area turns into an encouraging sign. The outcome of catastrophic events frequently witnesses networks mobilizing together, showing a strength brought into the world from shared bonds, common help, and an aggregate assurance to revamp.

The worldwide size of difficulties, for example, environmental change, pandemics, and financial emergencies highlights the significance of aggregate versatility. Countries and worldwide networks face difficulties that rise above individual encounters. The capacity to team up, share assets, and answer on the whole to worldwide difficulties turns into a sign of strength on an excellent scale. In the interconnected universe of the 21st hundred years, the versatility of one country can have expanding influences, affecting the flexibility of others.

The representation of a stream catches the pith of flexibility — a unique stream that experiences deterrents, explores around them, and proceeds with its excursion towards the ocean. Streams don't stream in straight lines; they wander, adjust, and continue. Likewise, the excursion through mishaps includes exploring the exciting bends in the road of life, adjusting to unanticipated difficulties, and persevering with a feeling of direction.

Versatility isn't an objective; it is a continuous course of development and variation. The allegorical waterway of strength courses through the scene of human experience, forming the landscape it experiences. An excursion envelops both the back and forth movements, the rapids and quiet waters, mirroring the unique idea of life's difficulties.

The investigation of flexibility has led to the idea of post-horrendous development — a peculiarity where people recuperate from misfortunes as well as experience individual and mental development in the consequence. Mishaps become impetuses for groundbreaking change, driving people to rethink needs, develop new viewpoints, and track down importance even with affliction.

Think about the tale of Maria, an overcomer of a horrible mishap. In the result, Maria confronted the strenuous course of mending, attracting on her versatility to explore the close to home outcome. Through treatment, reflection, and backing, Maria recuperated from the injury as well as found a newly discovered feeling of direction. Her versatility changed the mishap into a chance for self-improvement, touching off an enthusiasm for backing and backing for others confronting comparable difficulties.

The connection among misfortunes and self-awareness isn't direct; it is nuanced and complex. People might confront misfortunes that at first appear to be unconquerable, just to find stowed away repositories of solidarity inside themselves. The extraordinary force of misfortunes lies in the potential for self-revelation, the reconsideration of needs, and the development of an additional true and enabled self.

In the domain of schooling, flexibility is a critical consider understudies' capacity to explore scholarly difficulties and misfortunes. The progress to advanced education, scholastic tensions, and the vulnerabilities representing things to come can present imposing impediments. Understudies who develop versatility abilities, for example, viable critical thinking, using time productively, and the capacity to look for help, are better prepared to conquer scholastic misfortunes and flourish in the learning climate.

Instructive foundations, perceiving the significance of flexibility, progressively integrate versatility incorporating programs into their educational plans. These projects mean to outfit understudies with scholarly abilities as well as the mental apparatuses expected to confront misfortunes. By cultivating versatility, instructive organizations add to the comprehensive advancement of understudies, setting them up for the intricacies of the expert and individual difficulties that lie ahead.

In the expert field, flexibility is an essential resource despite the steadily changing scene of the working environment. People who can adjust to new innovations, explore authoritative changes, and return from vocation mishaps are better situated for long haul achievement. The capacity to gain from disappointments, embrace change, and keep a positive mentality notwithstanding challenges turns into an upper hand in a quickly developing proficient scene.

Associations, as well, perceive the significance of a strong labor force. Versatile representatives add to a positive work environment culture, encouraging development, joint effort, and flexibility. In a period where employer stability is progressively unsure, the versatility of representatives turns into an essential resource for associations exploring the intricacies of the worldwide economy.

The convergence of innovation and strength is clear in the computerized age, where people and associations influence advanced devices to upgrade their ability to defeat mishaps. Online people group, virtual encouraging groups of people, and computerized assets give roads to people confronting mishaps to interface, share encounters, and access data. The computerized scene turns into a virtual pot for the development of strength, separating topographical hindrances and making worldwide organizations of help.

The exchange among flexibility and psychological well-being is a critical part of the human experience. Misfortunes, especially those of an individual or profound nature, can influence mental prosperity.

Flexibility turns into a defensive variable, buffering against the adverse consequences of stress, injury, and difficulty. The capacity to quickly return from difficulties adds to profound guideline, adapting abilities, and by and large mental prosperity.

On the other hand, emotional well-being difficulties can influence a singular's versatility, making a mind boggling interrelationship. People confronting psychological wellness issues might find it trying to explore misfortunes, and difficulties, thusly, can intensify emotional well-being battles. The reconciliation of emotional wellness support into strength building drives perceives the all encompassing nature of prosperity, recognizing that psychological well-being is a basic part of a singular's capacity to defeat misfortunes.

Social and cultural elements impact the articulation and development of flexibility. Various societies might underscore specific qualities, survival techniques, or backing structures that shape the versatility story. Cultural perspectives towards disappointment, the disgrace encompassing mishaps, and the accessibility of assets all add to the versatility environment inside a given local area.

In certain societies, the aggregate ethos puts serious areas of strength for an on common help and relationship. People might draw strength from affectionate informal organizations, familial bonds, and social practices that work with flexibility. Interestingly, individualistic societies might focus on confidence, individual organization, and autonomy as key parts of versatility.

The social and cultural elements of versatility highlight the significance of setting in understanding and encouraging strength. Mediations and drives pointed toward building flexibility should be socially delicate, recognizing the variety of human encounters and the one of a kind manners by which various networks explore mishaps.

The mission for flexibility is definitely not a one-size-fits-all undertaking; a profoundly private excursion unfurls with regards to individual encounters, cultural impacts, and social elements. The story of flexibility is written in the narratives of regular legends who face misfortunes with fortitude, versatility, and an enduring soul.

The figurative embroidery of strength winds around a story that rises above the limits of time, geology, and culture. It is a general story — a demonstration of the human soul's ability to rise like a phoenix after difficulties, changed and fortified by the excursion. The strings of versatility interface the person to the group, making a dynamic mosaic of shared strength that resonates through the passages of mankind's set of experiences.

All in all, strength remains as a critical consider beating difficulties, a unique power that shapes the human excursion through difficulty. The narratives of people, networks, and associations exploring misfortunes uncover the groundbreaking influence of versatility — an influence that exists in every individual, ready to be gathered in the pot of difficulties.

As the stream of versatility keeps on moving through the scene of human experience, its ebbs and flows convey with them the examples of flexibility, strength, and the getting through human ability to conquer difficulties and arise more grounded on the opposite side.

5.2 Strategies for bouncing back from injuries or setbacks

In the domain of human experience, difficulties and wounds are unavoidable sidekicks on the excursion of life. Whether physical, profound, or proficient, difficulties can possibly upset the course of one's presence. Be that as it may, the capacity to return from such provokes is a demonstration of the strength intrinsic in the human soul. In investigating methodologies for quickly returning from wounds or difficulties, we dive into the complexities of adapting, adjusting, and at last winning over affliction.

Actual wounds, frequently unforeseen and troublesome, can present critical difficulties to a singular's prosperity. The course of recuperation includes actual recovery as well as a psychological and profound excursion towards reclamation. Procedures for returning quickly from actual wounds incorporate a comprehensive methodology, tending to both the substantial parts of recuperating and the elusive parts of mental guts.

The underlying period of adapting to an actual physical issue is frequently set apart by shock, dissatisfaction, and a feeling of misfortune. People might wrestle with the abrupt interruption to their day to day schedules, the restrictions forced by the injury, and the vulnerability encompassing the recuperation cycle. In this stage, recognizing and handling the feelings related with the mishap turns into a significant initial step.

The significance of everyday reassurance couldn't possibly be more significant during the beginning phases of injury recuperation. Companions, family, and an encouraging group of people give an important wellbeing net, offering figuring out, compassion, and consolation. This basic encouragement reduces sensations of seclusion as well as establishes the groundwork for flexibility — a critical consider returning from misfortunes.

One of the crucial methodologies for actual injury recuperation is the foundation of an extensive restoration plan. This arrangement, frequently created as a team with medical care experts, frames the means, activities, and courses of events for the recuperation cycle. A very much organized restoration plan tends to the actual parts of recuperating as well as encourages a feeling of organization and command over one's recuperation process.

Exercise based recuperation assumes a focal part in recovery, zeroing in on reestablishing versatility, strength, and adaptability. The organization between the individual and the medical services group turns into a cooperative exertion, with the individual effectively taking part in their recuperation. The obligation to the endorsed activities and treatments contributes not exclusively to actual recuperating yet in addition to the development of discipline and steadiness.

Taking on an outlook of slow advancement is essential to returning quickly from actual wounds. While the longing for a quick recuperation is normal, it is fundamental to perceive that mending requires some investment. Setting sensible assumptions and celebrating gradual accomplishments add to an uplifting perspective, forestalling demoralization even with apparent sluggish advancement.

Notwithstanding actual recovery, mental versatility is a foundation of returning from wounds. Mind-body strategies like care, reflection, and perception become significant devices in overseeing torment, decreasing pressure, and cultivating a positive mental disposition. The brain's impact on the body's mending processes highlights the interconnected idea of physical and mental prosperity.

The job of objective setting in injury recuperation is multi-layered. Past the overall objective of actual reclamation, setting more modest, feasible achievements gives a guide to advance. These achievements might envelop explicit actual accomplishments, like better scope of movement or expanded strength, as well as mental achievements, for example, beating dread or nervousness related with the injury.

Versatile methods for dealing with hardship or stress, like humor, good faith, and appreciation, add to the mental flexibility expected to explore the difficulties of actual wounds. Humor, specifically, can act as a strong survival technique, offering a happy viewpoint on the circumstance and encouraging a feeling of flexibility despite difficulty. Positive thinking, grounded in a faith in one's capacity to beat difficulties, turns into a main impetus for proceeded with exertion and steadiness.

The most common way of quickly returning from actual wounds isn't exclusively a singular undertaking; it frequently includes joint effort with medical care experts, restoration trained professionals, and a more extensive encouraging group of people. Viable correspondence with the medical care group, clarifying some pressing issues, and looking for explanation about the recuperation cycle engage people to take part in their mending process effectively. The cooperative energy between individual exertion and expert direction makes a hearty starting point for fruitful recuperation.

With regards to profound or mental difficulties, the methodologies for returning frequently share shared characteristics with those utilized in actual injury recuperation. Close to home mishaps, whether coming from individual connections, vocation challenges, or existential emergencies, require a complex methodology that includes self-reflection, consistent encouragement, and versatile strategies for dealing with especially difficult times.

Self-reflection fills in as a beginning stage for people confronting profound mishaps. Finding opportunity to introspect, recognize the main drivers of trouble, and comprehend one's personal reactions lays the basis for viable survival techniques.

The act of self-reflection encourages the capacity to understand people on a profound level — a critical part of strength even with difficulties.

Consistent reassurance, similar to its job in actual injury recuperation, stays central in exploring close to home misfortunes. The demonstration of discussing one's thoughts with confided in companions, relatives, or psychological wellness experts gives an outlet to articulation, approval, and viewpoint. Basic reassurance networks become secures in the tempest, offering a place of refuge for people to process and recuperate.

Mental conduct methodologies, established in the comprehension of the transaction between considerations, sentiments, and ways of behaving, offer significant devices for returning from profound mishaps. Testing pessimistic idea designs, reexamining mutilated convictions, and developing a more adjusted viewpoint add to profound strength. These procedures enable people to explore difficulties with more noteworthy flexibility and a better mentality.

The act of self-empathy arises as a strong system for conquering close to home mishaps. Self-sympathy includes treating oneself with consideration, remembering one's common humankind, and embracing defects. Despite mishaps, self-sympathy turns into a delicate directing power, permitting people to explore difficulties with a feeling of understanding and confidence.

Versatile survival strategies, for example, critical thinking, looking for proficient direction, and participating in exercises that give pleasure, add to close to home strength. The capacity to move toward difficulties with an answer situated outlook, combined with an eagerness to look for help when required, improves one's ability to return quickly from close to home mishaps.

In the expert domain, mishaps, for example, employment misfortune, profession changes, or business disappointments can especially challenge. The methodologies for returning expertly include a mix of versatility, flexibility, and vital preparation. The profession scene, portrayed by its dynamic nature, requests a proactive way to deal with misfortunes and a readiness to embrace change.

Organizing, both face to face and on the web, assumes a significant part in proficient versatility. Fabricating and keeping a hearty expert organization gives admittance to open doors as well as offers a wellspring of help and direction during misfortunes. The cooperative idea of systems administration lines up with the thought that proficient achievement frequently depends on the strength of relational associations.

Consistent mastering and expertise advancement add to proficient strength. In a consistently developing position market, people who focus on keeping up to date with industry patterns, procuring new abilities, and developing a development mentality position themselves for

progress in spite of misfortunes. The capacity to adjust to changing proficient scenes turns into a vital resource in quickly returning from vocation challenges.

Enterprising mishaps, like business disappointments or monetary difficulties, require a remarkable arrangement of systems for recuperation. Versatility in the enterprising domain includes a mix of flexibility, key examination, and an eagerness to gain from disappointments. Business visionaries frequently wrestle with the innate vulnerability of undertakings, and the capacity to return lays on the ability to explore vagueness with versatility.

Vital preparation, including an intensive examination of the variables adding to misfortunes, shapes a foundation of expert versatility. Business visionaries and experts the same advantage from an exhaustive evaluation of the circumstance, recognizing regions for development, and devising an essential strategy for pushing ahead. This ground breaking approach lays the preparation for flexibility and future achievement.

Monetary mishaps, whether coming about because of monetary slumps, unforeseen costs, or poor monetary choices, require an insightful and vital reaction. Making a reasonable spending plan, looking for monetary counsel, and investigating elective revenue streams are down to earth advances people can take to return quickly from monetary difficulties. The capacity to adjust one's monetary system to changing conditions is characteristic of monetary strength.

Notwithstanding difficulties, the reception of a development outlook turns out to be especially important. The development attitude, grounded in the conviction that capacities and knowledge can be created through devotion and difficult work, cultivates strength despite proficient difficulties. Embracing difficulties as any open doors for learning, development, and development turns into a core value for progress.

The worldwide scene, set apart by difficulties, for example, environmental change, pandemics, and international vulnerabilities, highlights the significance of cultural flexibility. Methodologies for returning from cultural difficulties include aggregate endeavors, versatile administration, and a common obligation to supportability and inclusivity.

Cultural versatility is firmly connected to the strength of social foundations, local area attachment, and versatile administration structures. Networks that put resources into social foundation, encourage comprehensive strategies, and focus on the prosperity of their individuals are better prepared to climate cultural difficulties. The capacity to adjust administration designs to changing conditions becomes essential in encouraging cultural versatility.

Environmental change, a perplexing and interconnected challenge, requires methodologies for both relief and transformation. Moderation endeavors include diminishing ozone harming substance outflows, changing to environmentally friendly power sources, and cultivating economical practices.

Transformation techniques center around building versatile networks, creating framework that can endure natural changes, and safeguarding weak populaces from the effects of environmental change.

Pandemic strength includes a mix of vigorous medical care frameworks, successful emergency the executives, and a worldwide cooperative reaction. The illustrations gained from worldwide wellbeing emergencies underline the significance of readiness, data sharing, and impartial admittance to medical care assets. The capacity to adjust general wellbeing techniques continuously turns into an essential consider beating pandemics.

Even with international vulnerabilities, methodologies for cultural flexibility revolve around strategy, coordinated effort, and compromise. Building solid worldwide associations, participating in strategic exchange, and cultivating social comprehension add to worldwide security. The capacity to explore international provokes with strength includes a guarantee to exchange, strategy, and the quest for tranquil arrangements.

The crossing point of innovation and cultural flexibility is obvious in the computerized age. Computerized devices and correspondence advances assume a crucial part in emergency reaction, data scattering, and encouraging worldwide network. In any case, the difficulties acted by issues such like online protection, information security, and advanced separates highlight the requirement for moral and comprehensive ways to deal with mechanical development.

5.3 Learning from failures and turning them into opportunities for growth

In the many-sided embroidery of the human experience, disappointments are unavoidable as well as are additionally strong pots for development, learning, and flexibility. The capacity to gather examples from disappointments and change them into potential open doors for individual and expert improvement is a sign of people who explore the complicated landscape of existence with shrewdness and flexibility. This investigation digs into the significant bits of knowledge implanted in the excursion of gaining from disappointments, enlightening the extraordinary power that emerges when mishaps are embraced as venturing stones as opposed to hindrances.

Disappointments, whether enormous or little, are an inborn piece of the human excursion. They manifest in different domains — scholastic undertakings, vocation pursuits, relational connections, and individual objectives. The most important phase in transforming disappointments into open doors for development lies in developing a mentality that reexamines misfortunes as significant encounters as opposed to impossible deterrents. This change in context is primary to the most common way of gaining from disappointments, impelling people toward a way of self-disclosure and ceaseless improvement.

The profound scene following a disappointment is frequently set apart by dissatisfaction, disappointment, and a serious insecurity. Recognizing and handling these feelings is a vital part of the learning venture. As opposed to stifling or keeping away from these sentiments, people are urged to go up against and embrace them. It is inside the pot of these feelings that the seeds of strength are planted — a versatility that turns into the bedrock for changing disappointments into impetuses for development.

Self-reflection arises as a powerful device for removing bits of knowledge from disappointments. In the result of difficulties, people are urged to take part in reflection, posing examining inquiries about the variables that added to the disappointment. What were the hidden suspicions? Were there holes in information or expertise? Did outer variables assume a part? By digging into the main drivers, people gain a more profound comprehension of the elements at play, preparing for designated procedures to address and defeat future difficulties.

Gaining from disappointments is a powerful cycle that includes grasping the 'what' as well as the 'why' and 'how.' The investigation stretches out past superficial examination, empowering people to disentangle the complexities of their dynamic cycles, critical thinking draws near, and relational elements. This profundity of understanding changes disappointments into rich storehouses of information, giving nuanced experiences that illuminate future activities and choices.

An essential part of gaining from disappointments is the acknowledgment that misfortunes are not inseparable from individual insufficiency. Disappointment doesn't characterize an individual; rather, it enlightens explicit parts of a circumstance or move toward that require refinement. This decoupling of self-esteem from the result of a specific undertaking is freeing and cultivates a development situated mentality — one that sees disappointments as impermanent mishaps on the way to dominance.

Disappointment frequently fills in as a strong impetus for development and imagination. In the cauldron of mishaps, people are provoked to figure outside the traditional limits, to investigate elective methodologies, and to challenge laid out standards. The historical backdrop of advanced developments, logical revelations, and imaginative magnum opuses is loaded with cases where disappointments went about as the maternity specialists of advancement. Gaining from disappointments turns into a powerful course of variation, emphasis, and the quest for novel arrangements.

The idea of a 'development outlook,' promoted by clinician Ditty Dweck, is especially pertinent with regards to gaining from disappointments. A development outlook includes the conviction that capacities and knowledge can be created through commitment and difficult work. People with a development mentality view disappointments as any open doors to learn, develop, and upgrade their abilities. This viewpoint encourages strength, persistence, and a proactive way to deal with conquering misfortunes.

Transforming disappointments into open doors for development includes extricating the illustrations as well as the qualities and abilities that arose during the cycle. Recognizing the viewpoints wherein people exhibited strength, assurance, imagination, or powerful critical thinking during a mishap supports a positive self-story. This affirmation of qualities turns into a wellspring of strengthening, adding to a feeling of organization notwithstanding future difficulties.

Gaining from disappointments is definitely not a lone undertaking; it frequently includes looking for outside points of view and input. Productive criticism, whether from tutors, peers, or confided in consultants, gives important experiences that may be ignored in individual self-reflection. The readiness to request and consolidate criticism exhibits lowliness, a vital characteristic in the excursion of consistent learning and improvement.

The idea of 'bombing forward' exemplifies that disappointments are not relapses yet rather steps ahead loaded down with illustrations. Embracing the idea of bombing forward includes a mentality shift where disappointments are rethought as fundamental pieces of the excursion toward progress. Every difficulty turns into a venturing stone, pushing people forward with recently discovered experiences, strength, and a more profound comprehension of themselves.

Gaining from disappointments reaches out past the singular domain to the elements of groups and associations. In the expert scene, misfortunes are unavoidable, and the aggregate capacity to change disappointments into open doors for development turns into a competitive edge. Associations that encourage a culture of mental security, where people feel open to facing challenges and recognizing disappointments, establish a climate helpful for development and consistent improvement.

Group elements assume a vital part in the growing experience following disappointments. Empowering open correspondence, cooperation, and a common obligation to gaining from difficulties cultivate an aggregate versatility that impels the group forward. The post-op interview process, where groups by and large examine disappointments, extricate examples, and plan for development, turns into a foundation of hierarchical learning and improvement.

Hierarchical pioneers, as stewards of culture and vision, assume a urgent part in forming the story around disappointments. Pioneers who model a development outlook, transparently recognize their own errors, and view mishaps as any open doors for hierarchical learning set the vibe for a culture that embraces nonstop improvement. The straightforwardness and modesty showed by pioneers even with disappointments add to a versatile and versatile hierarchical culture.

Development and imagination flourish in conditions where the feeling of dread toward disappointment is alleviated. Associations that view disappointments as significant input instead of as justification for discipline make a mentally place of refuge for people to face challenges, try, and contribute inventive thoughts.

This social shift changes disappointments into a wellspring of inspiration as opposed to a reason for dread, empowering a mentality of investigation and trial and error.

The idea of a 'learning association,' presented by Peter Senge, underlines the significance of ceaseless learning and variation in the hierarchical setting. Learning associations view disappointments as any open doors to further develop processes, upgrade execution, and adjust systems to advancing difficulties. The five disciplines of a learning association — individual dominance, mental models, shared vision, group learning, and frameworks thinking — give an all encompassing structure to utilizing disappointments as impetuses for development.

The crossing point of man-made consciousness (simulated intelligence) and gaining from disappointments acquaints an intriguing aspect with the conversation. AI calculations, a subset of computer based intelligence, depend on immense datasets that incorporate the two triumphs and disappointments. The iterative course of refining calculations through gaining from disappointments reflects the human growing experience, but on a sped up scale. The collaboration among human and AI highlights the powerful idea of utilizing misfortunes for ceaseless improvement.

Gaining from disappointments is a long lasting excursion that stretches out past expert and individual domains to the more extensive setting of cultural difficulties. Worldwide issues, for example, environmental change, general wellbeing emergencies, and financial abberations request aggregate learning and transformation. The capacity of social orders to change disappointments into open doors for development includes a guarantee to foundational change, development, and a common vision for a stronger and manageable future.

Ecological manageability gives a strong illustration of the cultural basic to gain from disappointments. Difficulties in tending to ecological difficulties, like strategy disappointments, impractical practices, and worldwide inaction, require a reconsideration of approaches. Gaining from these disappointments includes moving to eco-accommodating practices as well as tending to the underlying drivers of natural debasement through fundamental change and worldwide joint effort.

General wellbeing emergencies, exemplified by the difficulties presented by pandemics, underline the requirement for persistent learning and variation at the cultural level. The reaction to a general wellbeing emergency includes quick measures for control as well as an intelligent examination of the disappointments and weaknesses in readiness and reaction. Gaining from these disappointments illuminates procedures for building strong medical care frameworks, worldwide joint effort, and proactive measures to forestall future emergencies.

Civil rights developments, upholding for balance and basic liberties, embody the cultural excursion of gaining from disappointments. Mishaps chasing equity, whether as foundational separation, strategy disappointments, or cultural obstruction.

Chapter 6

Sculpting the Body: Training Techniques

Chiseling the body is a diverse excursion that incorporates a bunch of preparing strategies intended to improve strength, adaptability, and in general actual prosperity. Chasing a finely tuned physical make-up, people investigate different roads, from customary weightlifting to state of the art wellness patterns. This all encompassing way to deal with body chiseling includes the actual part of preparing as well as the psychological and profound parts that add to a fair and sound way of life.

At the center of body chiseling lies opposition preparing, a central procedure that has endured everyday hardship. Weightlifting, whether with free loads, machines, or obstruction groups, stays a foundation of solidarity improvement. This strategy includes exposing muscles to outside obstruction, inciting them to adjust and develop further over the long haul. The standards of moderate over-burden direct that as the body adjusts to a specific degree of obstruction, the heap should be expanded to keep invigorating muscle development.

Compound activities, like squats, deadlifts, and seat squeezes, stand as support points inside the domain of opposition preparing. These developments draw in various muscle bunches at the same time, encouraging proficiency and viability in a gym routine daily practice. Squats, for example, initiate the quadriceps, hamstrings, glutes, and center, giving an extensive lower body exercise. Deadlifts focus on the back chain, including the lower back, hamstrings, and glutes, advancing by and large strength and dependability. Seat presses draw in the chest, shoulders, and rear arm muscles, adding to chest area strength and muscle advancement.

Related to opposition preparing, cardiovascular activity assumes a vital part in chiseling the body and working on generally speaking wellness. Cardiovascular exercises, like running, cycling, and swimming, raise the pulse, advancing cardiovascular wellbeing and calorie use. Extreme cardio exercise (HIIT) has acquired unmistakable quality for its effectiveness in consuming calories and working on cardiovascular wellness in a more limited measure of time. This approach includes shifting back and forth between times of extraordinary effort and brief recuperation spans, provoking the body to adjust to fluctuating forces.

Adaptability, frequently eclipsed by its partners, is a critical component in body chiseling. Integrating extending activities and yoga into a wellness routine improves adaptability, joint portability, and scope of movement. These practices not just forestall wounds by advancing gracefulness in muscles and joints yet additionally add to generally solid equilibrium. An adaptable body is better prepared to perform different activities with legitimate structure, lessening the gamble of strain or injury.

Mind-body association arises as a critical part of body chiseling, underscoring the significance of mental concentration and focus during exercises. Practices, for example, care reflection and yoga urge people to interface with their bodies, cultivating a more profound consciousness of development designs, muscle commitment, and by and large actual sensations. This elevated mindfulness adds to more readily shape during works out, lessening the probability of wounds and improving the viability of the exercise.

Sustenance shapes the foundation of any fruitful body chiseling attempt. The saying "for getting healthy, the kind of food you eat is everything" turns out as expected as the body depends on a decent and supplement rich eating regimen to fuel exercises, support muscle development, and help in recuperation. Protein, a macronutrient pivotal for muscle fix and union, becomes the overwhelming focus in the eating regimen of people meaning to shape their bodies. Sources like lean meats, dairy, eggs, and plant-based choices give the essential amino acids to ideal muscle capability.

Carbs act as the body's essential energy source, powering extreme exercises and renewing glycogen stores. Entire grains, organic products, and vegetables offer complex sugars that support energy levels over the course of the day. Solid fats, got from sources like avocados, nuts, and olive oil, assume a part in chemical creation and by and large prosperity.

Legitimate hydration is similarly fundamental, supporting ideal execution, supplement transport, and the body's regular detoxification processes.

Periodization, a precise way to deal with preparing, includes spinning through various stages to forestall levels and upgrade results. These stages might incorporate times of extreme focus preparing, hypertrophy-centered exercises, and dynamic recuperation. By differing the preparation upgrade, the body is consistently tested, advancing variation and development. Periodization additionally takes into account key deload stages, decreasing preparation volume to forestall burnout and improve long haul maintainability.

Body chiseling reaches out past the limits of the exercise center, enveloping way of life decisions that influence in general wellbeing and wellness. Adequate and quality rest is an essential part, as it upholds recuperation, chemical guideline, and mental capability. Persistent lack of sleep can block progress in body chiseling by obstructing muscle recuperation and expanding the gamble of wounds. Stress the board procedures, like contemplation, profound breathing activities, or side interests, add to generally speaking prosperity and emphatically impact actual results.

The joining of innovation into body chiseling has introduced another period of customized and information driven wellness. Wearable wellness trackers, smartwatches, and portable applications permit people to screen different parts of their wellbeing and wellness venture. Following measurements, for example, pulse, calories consumed, and rest designs gives important experiences, empowering clients to come to informed conclusions about their preparation and recuperation systems.

Virtual wellness stages and web based training have acquired prominence, offering people the adaptability to get to directed exercises and master exhortation from the solace of their homes. These stages give an assorted scope of exercises, taking special care of various wellness levels, inclinations, and objectives. The openness of virtual preparation has democratized wellness, making master direction accessible to a more extensive crowd.

Practical preparation, established in developments that copy genuine exercises, has built up some forward movement in the body chiseling scene. This approach stresses practices that connect with numerous muscle gatherings and improve coordination, equilibrium, and dependability. Utilitarian preparation isn't just viable for everyday exercises yet additionally adds to a balanced and practical physical make-up. Practices like iron weight swings, medication ball tosses, and bodyweight developments fall under the umbrella of utilitarian preparation.

The social part of wellness can't be disregarded, as local area commitment and backing assume a fundamental part in keeping up with inspiration and adherence to a wellness routine. Bunch wellness classes, whether face to face or virtual, encourage a feeling of brotherhood and responsibility.

Wellness people group via web-based entertainment stages give a space to people to share their excursions, look for exhortation, and celebrate accomplishments, establishing a strong and spurring climate.

Body chiseling is a dynamic and developing interaction, with patterns and advancements consistently molding the scene. Super advanced gear, for example, vibration stages and electrostimulation gadgets, guarantee to improve muscle enactment and speed up results. While these advances might offer extra roads for investigation, their viability and long haul influence on body chiseling remain subjects of progressing research.

The significance of legitimate method couldn't possibly be more significant in that frame of mind of body chiseling. Performing practices with right structure boosts their adequacy as well as limits the gamble of wounds. Looking for direction from wellness experts, whether face to face or through virtual training, guarantees that people get customized guidance and input to refine their method. Predictable and careful execution of activities adds to ideal outcomes and long haul progress in body chiseling.

The idea of body energy has acquired unmistakable quality, testing regular thoughts of the "ideal" physical make-up and advancing self-acknowledgment. Body chiseling, in this unique circumstance, turns into an excursion of personal growth and taking care of oneself as opposed to a quest for cultural principles. Embracing one's remarkable body shape and valuing the advancement accomplished, no matter what the scale, cultivates a positive and reasonable way to deal with wellness.

All in all, chiseling the body includes a comprehensive methodology that coordinates obstruction preparing, cardiovascular activity, adaptability, nourishment, and outlook. The cooperative energy of these components makes a far reaching and maintainable structure for accomplishing wellness objectives. Embracing the standards of periodization, integrating innovation capably, and esteeming the social and local area parts of wellness add to a balanced body chiseling venture.

As people leave on the way of body chiseling, it is fundamental to focus on well-being, prosperity, and self-acknowledgment. The excursion is exceptional for every individual, and the accentuation ought to be on progress, consistency, and a positive relationship with one's body. In the steadily developing scene of wellness, remaining educated, liberal, and versatile guarantees that people can explore the assorted exhibit of preparing procedures and find a methodology that lines up with their objectives and values. At last, chiseling the body isn't just about actual change; a comprehensive excursion envelops the psyche, body, and soul.

6.1 Introduction to different workout routines for strength and muscle building

Setting out on an excursion towards strength and muscle building includes exploring a huge range of gym routine schedules, each intended to target explicit parts of actual wellness. Whether you're a carefully prepared exercise center participant or a newbie to the universe of solidarity preparing, understanding the standards behind various exercise routine schedules is fundamental for making a viable and balanced wellness plan.

At the core of muscle building lies the standard of moderate over-burden. This principal idea states that muscles should be reliably exposed to expanding levels of protection from invigorate development. As people participate in obstruction preparing, whether through bodyweight works out, free loads, or machines, the body adjusts to the pressure put on the muscles by becoming more grounded and stronger.

One of the most well known and dependable gym routine schedules for muscle building is the exemplary parted daily practice. This approach includes partitioning the body into various muscle gatherings and preparing each gathering on independent days. Normal parts incorporate the chest and rear arm muscles, back and biceps, and legs. This technique takes into account engaged and extreme exercises focusing on unambiguous muscle gatherings, with more than adequate time for recuperation between meetings.

Full-body exercises offer an elective methodology, focusing on numerous muscle bunches in a solitary meeting. These schedules are portrayed by compound activities that connect enormous muscle gatherings, like squats, deadlifts, and seat presses. Full-body exercises are frequently suggested for novices or those with restricted time, as they give complete preparation in a consolidated configuration.

Push-pull gym routine schedules address a fair way to deal with muscle working by gathering practices in light of moving around developments. Push works out, for example, chest presses and shoulder presses, connect with muscles associated with pushing developments. Pull works out, including columns and pull-ups, center around muscles utilized in pulling activities. This technique guarantees a balanced improvement of contradicting muscle gatherings, advancing evenness and diminishing the gamble of uneven characters.

Extreme focus preparing, generally known as HIT, underscores brief and serious exercises to boost muscle excitement. HIT schedules frequently include lifting significant burdens for less redundancies, pushing the muscles to approach disappointment. This approach is established in the way of thinking that short, extreme eruptions of exertion can yield huge additions in strength and bulk.

Weight training, as a discipline, puts an essential spotlight on hypertrophy - the expansion in muscle size. Weight training exercise routine schedules commonly include a higher volume of activities and reiterations, underlining muscle detachment to target explicit regions. These schedules frequently consolidate strategies, for example, drop sets, supersets, and segregation activities to debilitate muscles and advance hypertrophy.

Powerlifting remains as opposed to working out, with an emphasis on crude strength instead of muscle size. Powerlifting exercises base on three essential lifts: squat, seat press, and deadlift. Preparing for powerlifting includes lifting significant burdens with lower reiterations to augment strength gains. The accentuation on these compound developments adds to generally speaking practical strength.

CrossFit, an extreme focus work out schedule, joins components of weightlifting, cardiovascular activity, and vaulting. CrossFit exercises, known as WODs (Exercises of the Day), shift everyday and challenge members with a blend of practical developments. The objective is to fabricate a wide and comprehensive wellness, incorporating strength, perseverance, and adaptability.

High-volume preparing includes playing out countless sets and reiterations, frequently with moderate loads. This approach intends to prompt muscle exhaustion and metabolic pressure, adding to muscle development. High-volume exercises are portrayed by a supported exertion over a drawn out span, advancing perseverance close by muscle improvement.

German Volume Preparing (GVT) is a specific type of high-volume preparing known for its power. GVT includes performing ten arrangements of ten reiterations for a solitary activity, zeroing in on a particular muscle bunch. This high-reiteration approach invigorates muscle strands and can prompt critical hypertrophy when executed with appropriate structure and force.

Hand weight and free weight buildings give a dynamic and time-proficient exercise routine daily schedule. These edifices include playing out a succession of activities with insignificant rest between developments. Hand weight buildings, for example, may incorporate a progression of activities like lines, squats, and presses. These schedules challenge both strength and cardiovascular wellness while advancing calorie use.

Practical wellness exercises focus on developments that copy genuine exercises, improving in general actual capacities. Practices frequently include multi-joint developments and draw in the center for strength. Practical exercises add to further developed coordination, equilibrium, and adaptability, making them important for people looking for strength and muscle as well as useful qualification for day to day exercises.

High-intensity aerobics includes traveling through a progression of practices in quick progression, commonly focusing on various muscle gatherings.

The ceaseless idea of high-intensity exercise keeps the pulse raised, consolidating strength preparing with cardiovascular advantages. This time-proficient methodology is reasonable for people with restricted time who need a thorough exercise.

Periodization, an idea referenced prior, includes decisively fluctuating preparation factors over the long haul to forestall levels and streamline results. Periodization can be applied to different gym routine schedules, permitting people to go through various periods of power, volume, and concentration. This orderly methodology guarantees a balanced and economical movement in strength and muscle building.

While the previously mentioned exercise routine schedules offer different ways to deal with accomplishing strength and muscle-building objectives, it's essential to take note of that singular inclinations, wellness levels, and explicit targets ought to direct the decision of a daily practice. Moreover, a balanced methodology that integrates components of obstruction preparing, cardiovascular activity, adaptability, and recuperation procedures is critical to accomplishing exhaustive wellness.

Chasing after strength and muscle building, focusing on appropriate structure and strategy is foremost. Wrong structure frustrates progress as well as expands the gamble of wounds. Looking for direction from wellness experts, whether through in-person training or virtual stages, gives important experiences into practice execution, program plan, and customized changes in view of individual necessities and capacities.

Sustenance assumes a significant part in supporting strength and muscle-building endeavors. Protein admission, specifically, is significant for muscle fix and development. Consuming a satisfactory measure of protein from sources like lean meats, dairy, eggs, and plant-based choices guarantees that the body has the essential structure blocks for muscle blend. Carbs and fats add to generally energy levels and give fundamental supplements to ideal execution.

Rest and recuperation are vital parts of any compelling strength and muscle-building program. Muscles need time to fix and develop further after serious exercises. Overtraining, described by exorbitant activity without sufficient recuperation, can prompt exhaustion, diminished execution, and expanded weakness to wounds.

Integrating rest days, appropriate rest, and unwinding procedures upholds the body's recuperation processes.

All in all, the universe of solidarity and muscle building offers a different cluster of gym routine schedules, each with its extraordinary methodology and advantages. From exemplary split schedules to extreme focus preparing, the key is to find a standard that lines up with individual objectives, inclinations, and wellness levels. Whether the emphasis is on hypertrophy, crude strength, or in general utilitarian wellness, a balanced methodology that incorporates legitimate sustenance, strategy, and recuperation techniques guarantees a practical and powerful excursion towards strength and muscle building.

6.2 Incorporating variety and intensity into training sessions

Accomplishing wellness objectives and keeping up with long haul inspiration requires a key and dynamic way to deal with preparing. Integrating assortment and power into instructional meetings is a central part of a balanced wellness routine. This complex procedure forestalls repetitiveness as well as difficulties the body in various ways, advancing persistent variation and improvement.

Assortment in instructional courses includes expanding the kinds of activities, preparing modalities, and exercise structures. This can envelop changes in the choice of activities, the request in which they are performed, or the gear utilized. By presenting assortment, people can target different muscle gatherings, development examples, and energy frameworks, keeping the body from leveling and upgrading generally speaking wellness.

One compelling method for imbuing assortment into instructional meetings is through the joining of various activity modalities. Conventional weightlifting works out, for example, squats and seat presses, can be supplemented with bodyweight practices like push-ups, pull-ups, and jumps. Coordinating practical developments that mirror genuine exercises, for example, iron weight swings or medication ball tosses, adds a powerful component to exercises.

The use of various preparation apparatuses additionally adds to assortment. Free loads, machines, obstruction groups, and dependability balls offer novel difficulties and connect with muscles in unmistakable ways. For instance, playing out a free weight seat press gives an unexpected boost in comparison to utilizing a chest press machine, as the adjustment expected with free loads enacts extra muscle filaments.

Integrating cardiovascular activities into instructional courses mixes it up. Running, cycling, paddling, or work out with rope meetings can be blended with obstruction preparing to make balanced exercises. Stop and go aerobic exercise (HIIT), which shifts back and forth between short eruptions of serious exertion and brief times of rest, is especially powerful for both cardiovascular wellness and calorie consumption.

The design of an exercise can likewise be changed to keep things fascinating and testing. While certain meetings might follow a customary set and reiteration plot, others can be coordinated as circuit exercises, with members traveling through a progression of activities with insignificant rest. This approach targets different muscle bunches as well as raises the pulse, giving cardiovascular advantages.

Periodization, as referenced prior, is a deliberate methodology that includes spinning through various periods of force and concentration. This idea lines up with integrating assortment into preparing. By isolating the preparation year into particular stages, like strength, hypertrophy, and perseverance, people can address explicit objectives while keeping away from the traps of overtraining and repetitiveness.

Power, then again, is a urgent component for evoking physiological variations and accomplishing wellness objectives. Force alludes to the amount of exertion applied during an exercise, and it tends to be controlled through variables like burden, redundancies, rest stretches, and by and large exercise length. A harmony between both assortment and power guarantees a balanced and viable preparation program.

Expanding the force of an exercise can be accomplished through moderate overburden - bit by bit expanding the obstruction, volume, or power of activities over the long run. This guideline provokes the body to adjust, advancing strength gains and muscle advancement. For weightlifting, this might include adding more weight to the bar, while for cardiovascular activities, it could mean speeding up or opposition.

Focused energy preparing (HIT) is a particular methodology that underscores short eruptions of maximal exertion. HIT can be applied to both opposition preparing and cardiovascular activities. For opposition preparing, this could include lifting significant burdens for less redundancies, pushing the muscles to approach disappointment. With regards to cardiovascular activity, run spans or serious cycling meetings epitomize HIT.

The idea of time under pressure (TUT) is one more technique to build the force of obstruction preparing. TUT alludes to the complete term that muscles are under load during an activity. Dialing back the rhythm of redundancies and zeroing in on controlled developments builds TUT, escalating the boost on the muscles and improving both strength and muscle perseverance.

Metabolic molding, frequently connected with intense cardio exercise, includes organized, brief term, extreme focus practices that target both vigorous and anaerobic energy frameworks. These exercises, some of the time alluded to as "metcons," lift the pulse and challenge the body's capacity to recuperate between extreme endeavors. Metabolic molding is powerful for working on cardiovascular wellness and consuming calories.

Pyramid preparing is a strategy that includes bit by bit expanding and afterward diminishing the force or volume of an activity. This can be applied to both opposition preparing and cardiovascular activities. For instance, in a pyramid set of squats, the singular beginnings with a lighter load for higher redundancies, continuously builds the weight, tops at the heaviest burden for a moderate number of reiterations, and afterward diminishes the weight once more.

Zeroing in on compound developments is a successful method for escalating exercises. Compound activities connect with various muscle bunches all the while, requiring more prominent energy use and advancing in general strength advancement. Squats, deadlifts, and above presses are instances of build developments that enlist huge muscle gatherings and hoist the pulse, adding to both strength and cardiovascular advantages.

Integrating force procedures, for example, drop sets and supersets, into an exercise can lift the test and invigorate extra muscle strands. Drop sets include playing out an activity until disappointment and afterward quickly decreasing the load to proceed with the set. Supersets include matching two activities with negligible in the middle between, focusing on various muscle gatherings and expanding the general force of the meeting.

High-volume preparing, portrayed by countless sets and redundancies, is one more method for expanding the power of exercises. While high volume is frequently connected with working out, it very well may be applied to different preparation objectives. Playing out various sets with moderate loads difficulties muscles and instigates metabolic pressure, adding to muscle development and perseverance.

The Tabata convention is a particular type of extreme cardio exercise that switches back and forth between 20 seconds of extraordinary exertion and 10 seconds of rest for a sum of four minutes. This organization can be applied to different activities, giving a period productive and extraordinary exercise. Tabata preparing is known for its adequacy in working on both vigorous and anaerobic wellness.

Mind-body association and mental center are vital parts of preparing force. Focusing on the nature of developments, keeping up with legitimate structure, and pushing through mental obstructions add to the general force of an exercise. Practices, for example, care reflection and perception procedures can improve the brain body association, cultivating a more profound familiarity with the preparation experience.

Periodizing power is an essential way to deal with forestall burnout and overtraining. Presenting periods of higher and lower power takes into account sufficient recuperation, decreasing the gamble of wounds and weariness. For instance, a strength-centered stage with significant burdens and lower reiterations can be trailed by a hypertrophy stage with moderate loads and higher redundancies.

It's critical to take note of that while power is fundamental for progress, balance is vital to forestall overtraining and advance long haul adherence. Satisfactory rest and recuperation periods, as well as paying attention to the body's signs, are fundamental parts of a practical and viable preparation program.

All in all, integrating assortment and force into instructional meetings is a dynamic and vital way to deal with accomplishing wellness objectives. By embracing different activity modalities, exercise designs, and power procedures, people can make a balanced and testing wellness routine. This forestalls weariness as well as animates consistent variation, advancing enhancements in strength, perseverance, and in general wellness. Offsetting assortment with force guarantees a maintainable and pleasant preparation experience, encouraging a long lasting obligation to wellbeing and prosperity.

6.3 Balancing cardiovascular exercise with strength training

Accomplishing an amicable harmony between cardiovascular activity and strength preparing is principal to far reaching wellness and generally prosperity. While the two modalities contribute particular advantages, incorporating them into a strong and vital wellness plan improves wellbeing results and upgrades actual execution. The collaboration of cardiovascular activity and strength preparing addresses different wellness objectives, from cardiovascular wellbeing and weight the board to muscle improvement and practical strength.

Cardiovascular activity, frequently alluded to as cardio, envelops exercises that raise the pulse and work on the proficiency of the cardiovascular framework. Running, cycling, swimming, lively strolling, and vigorous classes are instances of cardiovascular exercises that connect enormous muscle gatherings and increment oxygen utilization. These activities upgrade cardiovascular perseverance, help lung limit, and add to the effective vehicle of oxygen and supplements all through the body.

Strength preparing, then again, centers around obstruction practices intended to further develop muscle strength, power, and perseverance. This methodology incorporates lifting loads, performing bodyweight works out, and using obstruction groups or machines. Strength preparing advances the improvement of slender bulk, upholds bone wellbeing, and upgrades useful limit, permitting people to perform everyday exercises effortlessly.

The coordination of cardiovascular activity and strength preparing offers an all encompassing way to deal with wellness, tending to both the high-impact and anaerobic parts of actual work. Adjusting these two modalities requires cautious thought of individual objectives, wellness levels, and inclinations, as well as a comprehension of how they complete one another to make a synergistic impact.

Cardiovascular activity is prestigious for its effect on cardiovascular wellbeing, including the improvement of heart and lung capability. Participating in ordinary cardio exercises improves the heart's capacity to siphon blood productively, decreases resting pulse, and adds to bring down circulatory strain. Furthermore, cardiovascular activity assumes a critical part in diminishing the gamble of constant illnesses, like coronary illness, diabetes, and heftiness.

Weight the executives and calorie use are likewise huge advantages of cardiovascular activity. Exercises like running, cycling, and stop and go aerobic exercise (HIIT) consume calories and add to a negative energy balance, working with weight reduction or weight support. The metabolic impacts of cardio reach out past the exercise meeting, with expanded calorie utilization proceeding with during rest periods.

Cardiovascular activity further expands mental prosperity by advancing the arrival of endorphins, the body's regular state of mind enhancers.

Standard cooperation in cardio exercises is related with diminished side effects of tension and sadness, further developed rest quality, and upgraded mental capability. The mental advantages of cardio make it an important part of a comprehensive way to deal with wellbeing and wellness.

Strength preparing, then again, gives an extraordinary arrangement of advantages that supplements cardiovascular activity. One of the essential benefits is the improvement of slender bulk. Opposition preparing incites hypertrophy, the development of muscle filaments, adding to further developed body structure and metabolic proficiency. Expanded bulk likewise lifts the resting metabolic rate, working with weight the board.

The effect of solidarity preparing stretches out past feel, enveloping useful strength and upgraded execution in day to day exercises. Taking part in opposition practices further develops muscle strength, power, and perseverance, making undertakings, for example, lifting, conveying, and climbing steps more reasonable. This practical part of solidarity preparing is especially applicable for people looking to improve their by and large actual abilities.

Besides, strength preparing assumes a critical part in supporting bone wellbeing and diminishing the gamble of osteoporosis. Weight-bearing activities, incorporating those with opposition, invigorate bone development and increment bone thickness. This is particularly significant for people in danger of or overseeing osteoporosis, as strength preparing adds to skeletal strength and versatility.

The metabolic advantages of solidarity preparing supplement those of cardiovascular activity. While cardio exercises essentially add to calorie consuming during the exercise, strength preparing impacts post-practice energy use. The maintenance and recuperation processes following opposition exercises require energy, adding to a lengthy calorie consume even after the instructional course finishes up. This peculiarity is frequently alluded to as the afterburn impact or overabundance post-practice oxygen utilization (EPOC).

The blend of cardiovascular activity and strength preparing addresses a range of wellness objectives and advances generally speaking wellbeing. To find some kind of harmony between these modalities, people should think about their particular goals, time requirements, and inclinations. Here are key systems for coordinating and offsetting cardiovascular activity with strength preparing:

Lay out Clear Wellness Objectives:

Prior to planning a decent exercise routine daily practice, characterizing explicit wellness goals is urgent. Whether the emphasis is on weight reduction, muscle advancement, cardiovascular wellbeing, or generally prosperity, having clear targets directs the choice of activities and the portion of time to every methodology.

Make a Balanced Exercise Timetable:

A reasonable methodology includes consolidating both cardiovascular and strength instructional meetings into the week after week exercise plan. This circulation guarantees that every methodology gets consideration, forestalling the disregard of one angle for the other. For instance, a timetable could incorporate three days of solidarity preparing and two days of cardiovascular activity each week.

Use Simultaneous Preparation:

Simultaneous preparation includes consolidating cardiovascular activity and strength preparing inside a similar exercise meeting. This approach is effective for people with time limitations and can be custom-made to explicit objectives. For example, integrating stop and go aerobic exercise (HIIT) with bodyweight practices gives a period productive and compelling method for tending to both high-impact and anaerobic parts.

Shift back and forth Among Cardio and Strength Days:

A substitute methodology includes committing explicit days to either cardiovascular activity or strength preparing. This takes into account engaged and committed exercises for every methodology, forestalling weariness and advancing execution. For example, cardio exercises can be booked on Mondays, Wednesdays, and Fridays, while strength instructional courses happen on Tuesdays and Thursdays.

Integrate Full-Body Exercises:

Full-body exercises connect with both the upper and lower body, giving a far reaching preparing boost. These exercises frequently include compound activities that focus on different muscle bunches all the while. Full-body exercises can be especially compelling for people looking for a decent way to deal with wellness, as they address both cardiovascular and strength parts in a solitary meeting.

Decisively Join Cardio and Strength Meetings:

While planning an exercise plan, consider the succession of cardio and strength meetings. A few people favor beginning with cardiovascular activity to raise the pulse and warm up the body prior to changing to strength preparing. Others might decide on strength preparing first to focus on muscle improvement prior to finishing up with a cardio part.

Change Force and Term:

The force and term of both cardiovascular and strength instructional courses can be changed in light of individual objectives and inclinations. For instance, people going for the gold might underscore focused energy cardio meetings, while those zeroed in on muscle advancement might consolidate heavier loads and lower redundancies in their solidarity preparing schedule.

Periodize Preparing:

Periodization includes going through various periods of preparing, changing force, volume, and concentration. This essential methodology forestalls levels, limits the gamble of overtraining, and takes into account designated transformations. For example, a preparation cycle might incorporate a strength-centered stage followed by a cardiovascular accentuation, making a balanced and moderate program.

Pay attention to the Body:

Individual reactions to preparing differ, and it's fundamental to pay attention to the body's signs. Satisfactory rest, recuperation, and adaptability in the exercise plan add to long haul supportability. On the off chance that exhaustion or indications of overtraining arise, changes can be made to the force, recurrence, or span of meetings.

Consolidate Modalities Inventively:

Imagination in consolidating cardiovascular and strength practices changes up exercises. For example, high-intensity aerobics can include switching back and forth between cardio stretches, like hopping jacks or runs, and strength practices like squats or push-ups. This gives a different preparation boost as well as keeps up with commitment and inspiration.

Incorporate Dynamic Recuperation:

Dynamic recuperation meetings, like light running, swimming, or yoga, can be incorporated between additional serious exercises. These meetings work with recuperation, advance adaptability, and add to generally speaking prosperity. Dynamic recuperation additionally forestalls burnout and guarantees that the body is prepared for resulting instructional meetings.

Look for Proficient Direction:

Talking with wellness experts, like fitness coaches or exercise physiologists, can give customized direction. These specialists can evaluate individual wellness levels, tailor exercises to explicit objectives, and give experiences into successful and adjusted preparing systems.

Practice is a complex undertaking including a different exhibit of modalities, each contributing interestingly to actual wellbeing and prosperity. Strength preparing, a foundation of viable activity, centers around opposition based exercises intended to improve muscle strength, perseverance, and by and large useful limit. Coordinating different types of activity with strength preparing makes a far reaching and adjusted approach, tending to cardiovascular wellbeing, adaptability, and by and large wellness. This comprehensive viewpoint perceives the cooperative energies between various activity modalities, cultivating a balanced wellness routine.

Strength preparing, normally connected with weightlifting, includes the utilization of protection from challenge muscles and actuate transformations. This obstruction can emerge out of different sources, including free loads, machines, opposition groups, or even one's body weight.

The essential objective of solidarity preparing is to invigorate muscle development, work on strong strength, and upgrade the body's capacity to perform regular exercises.

Opposition preparing gives a horde of advantages past the improvement of solid strength. Worked on bone thickness, joint wellbeing, and metabolic capability are among the positive results related with standard strength preparing. Furthermore, obstruction practices add to expanded calorie consumption, making them an important part of weight the executives and generally speaking wellness.

Integrating cardiovascular activity close by strength preparing intensifies the advantages of the two modalities. Cardiovascular exercises, like running, cycling, and swimming, raise the pulse, advancing cardiovascular wellbeing, calorie consuming, and further developed perseverance. Consolidating these vigorous activities with strength preparing makes a synergistic impact, improving generally speaking wellness and giving a balanced way to deal with actual prosperity.

A decent work-out routine frequently incorporates a mix of cardiovascular activity and strength preparing, supplemented by adaptability and portability works out. This exhaustive methodology tends to various parts of wellness, advancing cardiovascular wellbeing, solid strength, adaptability, and generally speaking practical limit. Here are key parts of an activity routine that incorporates strength preparing with different modalities:

1. **Cardiovascular Activity:**
   Cardiovascular activity, ordinarily known as cardio, is an imperative part of a balanced work-out daily schedule. It includes exercises that hoist the pulse and work on cardiovascular wellbeing. Running, running, cycling, swimming, and vigorous classes are well known types of cardiovascular activity. Incorporating cardio meetings into an exercise routine adds to further developed perseverance, calorie consuming, and upgraded cardiovascular capability.
2. **Extreme cardio exercise (HIIT):**
   HIIT is a type of cardiovascular activity portrayed by short explosions of extreme exertion followed by brief times of rest or lower-power movement. This approach is time-proficient and viable for calorie consuming, cardiovascular wellness, and metabolic advantages. Joining strength preparing with HIIT makes a powerful exercise that challenges both the cardiovascular and solid frameworks.
3. **Adaptability and Portability Activities:**
   Adaptability and portability are fundamental parts of a balanced work-out everyday practice. Extending activities, yoga, and portability drills improve joint scope of movement, lessen the gamble of wounds, and add to generally speaking adaptability. Counting these activities close by strength preparing cultivates a reasonable way to deal with wellness, tending to both solid strength and joint adaptability.
4. **Useful Developments:**
   Useful developments emulate genuine exercises and draw in various muscle bunches all the while. Integrating useful activities into an exercise routine upgrades in general utilitarian limit and supports regular developments. Models incorporate squats, jumps, deadlifts, and portable weight swings. These activities add to further developed strength, dependability, and coordination.
5. **Center Fortifying Activities:**
   A solid center is major for in general soundness and utilitarian development. Center activities, like boards, Russian turns, and leg raises, focus on the muscles of the mid-region, lower back, and pelvis. Coordinating center reinforcing practices with strength preparing advances a steady and adjusted build, diminishing the gamble of back torment and upgrading stance.
6. **Equilibrium and Solidness Preparing:**
   Equilibrium and soundness preparing include practices that challenge the

body's capacity to keep up with balance. This type of preparing is especially gainful for more established grown-ups, as it diminishes the gamble of falls and upgrades generally strength. Consolidating balance works out, for example, single-leg stands or soundness ball works out, supplements strength preparing and adds to a balanced wellness schedule.

7. **Plyometric Activities:**
Plyometric practices include quick and hazardous developments, for example, box bounces, burpees, and hop squats. These activities upgrade power, readiness, and coordination. When joined with strength preparing, plyometrics add to an exhaustive way to deal with wellness, working on both solid strength and dynamic execution.

8. **Periodization:**
Periodization is an essential way to deal with preparing that includes pushing through various periods of force and concentration. This methodical variety forestalls levels, lessens the gamble of overtraining, and streamlines long haul progress. Periodization can be applied to both strength preparing and cardiovascular activity, taking into consideration designated transformations and proceeded with upgrades.

9. **Broadly educating:**
Broadly educating includes partaking in different exercises to forestall dreariness and decrease the gamble of abuse wounds. Participating in various types of cardiovascular activity, like cycling, swimming, or paddling, close by strength preparing brings variety into the daily practice. Broadly educating upgrades in general wellness as well as gives a psychological break from dull exercises.

10. **Mind-Body Association:**
Encouraging a brain body association is fundamental for ideal activity execution. Practices like care contemplation, yoga, or judo upgrade mindfulness, center, and mental strength. Consolidating mind-body rehearses close by strength preparing elevates an all encompassing way to deal with wellbeing, tending to both physical and mental prosperity.

11. **Recuperation Procedures:**
Incorporating recuperation procedures is urgent for keeping up with the maintainability of a work-out everyday practice. Satisfactory rest, legitimate hydration, and adequate rest add to by and large recuperation. Also, consolidating exercises like froth rolling, extending, or knead upholds muscle recuperation and lessens the gamble of wounds, considering reliable commitment to both strength preparing and cardiovascular activity.

12. **Practical Wellness Preparing:**
Practical wellness preparing underscores practices that duplicate genuine developments. These activities frequently include multi-joint developments and connect with the center for strength. Utilitarian wellness adds to worked on day

to day usefulness and is especially important for people looking for a commonsense and adjusted way to deal with wellness.

13. **Versatility and Movement:**
Work-out schedules ought to be versatile to individual requirements, inclinations, and wellness levels. Changing activities, changing force, and advancing progressively are fundamental parts of a reasonable methodology. This flexibility guarantees that the work-out routine remaining parts testing and charming, cultivating long haul adherence.

14. **Proficient Direction:**
Looking for direction from wellness experts, like fitness coaches or exercise physiologists, gives important bits of knowledge into making a customized and viable work-out daily practice. These specialists can evaluate individual wellness levels, address explicit objectives, and proposition direction on legitimate structure, strategy, and program plan.

15. **Consistency and Delight:**

Consistency is central in any work-out everyday practice. Laying out a normal that is charming and lines up with individual inclinations improves the probability of long haul adherence. Whether it's through bunch classes, open air exercises, or solo exercises, tracking down bliss in the work-out routine upgrades inspiration and maintainability.

Chapter 7

Fueling the Fire: Nutrition for Strength

In the persevering quest for actual strength, competitors and wellness devotees the same frequently end up exploring a complicated trap of preparing systems, recuperation techniques, and, maybe most critically, nourishing contemplations. The job of nourishment in improving strength, advancing muscle development, and upgrading generally execution couldn't possibly be more significant. It fills in as the fuel that controls the body's motor, supporting the requests of thorough preparation and working with the cycles that lead to expanded strength and versatility.

One of the basic standards of viable strength nourishment is understanding the energy prerequisites related with strength preparing. Strength competitors participate in extreme focus, anaerobic exercises that request huge energy consumption. The body depends on different energy frameworks, with the phosphagen framework being especially pertinent in brief length, extreme focus endeavors like truly difficult work. Creatine phosphate, put away in the muscles, gives quick energy during these extreme explosions of movement, stressing the significance of keeping up with ideal creatine levels through dietary sources or supplementation.

Sugars, frequently alluded to as the body's favored fuel source, assume a urgent part in strength-situated nourishment. The glycogen put away in muscles and the liver fills in as a promptly accessible energy source during exercise. Consuming a sufficient measure of sugars is fundamental for recharging glycogen stores, supporting energy levels, and supporting execution during strength instructional courses. Complex sugars, like entire grains and boring vegetables, give a supported arrival of energy, guaranteeing a steady blood glucose level all through the exercise.

Protein, one more foundation of solidarity nourishment, is irreplaceable for muscle fix, recuperation, and development. Strength preparing actuates microtears in muscle strands, and a satisfactory protein admission is essential for the union of new proteins, working with the maintenance cycle. The amino acids found in protein-rich food sources are the structure blocks of muscle tissue, making protein a non-debatable part of any strength-centered diet. Sources like lean meats, poultry, fish, eggs, and plant-based choices like beans and vegetables add to meeting the protein needs of people participated in strength preparing.

Chasing ideal strength, the significance of dietary fats ought not be neglected. Fats act as an energy save and are imperative for the retention of fat-solvent nutrients, for example, vitamin D, which assumes a part in bone wellbeing — a basic thought for strength competitors. Counting sound fats from sources like avocados, nuts, seeds, and olive oil in the eating routine can add to by and large prosperity and execution.

Hydration is a key part of solidarity sustenance that is frequently underrated. Drying out can weaken strength and power, compromise perseverance, and impede recuperation. Sufficient liquid admission is fundamental for keeping up with ideal execution and supporting physiological cycles like supplement transport, temperature guideline, and waste end. Electrolytes, which incorporate minerals like sodium, potassium, and magnesium, assume a critical part in liquid equilibrium and ought to be recharged, particularly after extraordinary instructional meetings that outcome in huge perspiration misfortune.

Timing is a basic aspect in strength nourishment, and the idea of supplement timing has acquired significant consideration. Consuming the ideal supplements at the perfect times can upgrade execution, support recuperation, and advance muscle development. Pre-exercise sustenance expects to give the energy important to the forthcoming instructional meeting and enhance supplement accessibility during exercise. A reasonable blend of sugars and a moderate measure of protein can be useful in such manner. Post-exercise nourishment, regularly known as the "anabolic window," centers around renewing glycogen stores, starting muscle protein combination, and advancing recuperation. A mix of quick processing sugars and great protein is many times suggested during this period.

Enhancements can be significant devices in the strength competitor's stockpile, yet they ought to supplement a balanced and supplement thick eating regimen as opposed to supplant it. Creatine monohydrate stands apart as one of the most investigated and compelling enhancements for strength and power upgrade. It expands the accessibility of phosphocreatine, adding to further developed execution during focused energy, brief length exercises. Spread chain amino acids (BCAAs) are another well known supplement, giving fundamental amino acids that help muscle protein amalgamation and diminish muscle protein breakdown. While enhancements can offer advantages, a mindful and informed approach is fundamental, taking into account individual requirements, objectives, and expected collaborations.

The idea of caloric excess or deficiency is fundamental to strength sustenance, contingent upon the singular's objectives. A caloric excess, where energy consumption surpasses use, is in many cases sought after by those going for the gold and strength gains. This excess gives the extra energy expected to muscle fix, recuperation, and development. Then again, a calorie deficiency, where energy consumption surpasses admission, is utilized for those looking for fat misfortune while expecting to safeguard bulk. The two methodologies require cautious thought of macronutrient dissemination and generally supplement thickness to guarantee that the body gets the fundamental components for ideal capability.

Adjusting the macronutrients — carbs, proteins, and fats — in the eating regimen is a nuanced and individualized process. The circulation of these macronutrients can be customized in light of elements like preparation force, length, and individual reaction. While there is nobody size-fits-all methodology, a common principle for strength competitors is to consume a sufficient measure of protein to help muscle upkeep and development, change sugar consumption in light of energy requests, and consolidate solid fats for by and large prosperity.

The job of micronutrients, including nutrients and minerals, ought to be acknowledged with a sober mind in strength sustenance. These micronutrients assume fundamental parts in energy digestion, resistant capability, and generally wellbeing. Vitamin D, for example, is significant for calcium retention and bone wellbeing, while zinc is engaged with protein blend and safe capability. A different and beautiful eating regimen that incorporates various products of the soil can add to addressing micronutrient needs. At times, supplementation might be justified to address explicit lacks or guarantee ideal levels, yet this ought to be finished under the direction of a medical services proficient.

The effect of nourishment on rest can't be neglected in that frame of mind of solidarity and athletic execution. Rest is a basic part of the recuperation interaction, and lacking or low quality rest can think twice about gains, obstruct recuperation, and increment the gamble of injury. Sustenance can impact rest quality through elements like the planning of feasts, the creation of the eating regimen, and the admission of rest advancing supplements.

Staying away from huge feasts near sleep time, directing caffeine consumption, and consolidating rest agreeable food sources like those wealthy in tryptophan and magnesium can add to more readily rest cleanliness.

The mental part of sustenance is a less unmistakable yet similarly significant aspect chasing strength. The connection among food and feelings, frequently alluded to as profound eating, can affect dietary decisions and, subsequently, execution. Stress, tension, and other profound elements can impact eating ways of behaving, prompting overconsumption or lacking supplement consumption. Fostering a solid and offset relationship with food, looking for help when required, and developing care around eating can add to a positive dietary outlook.

Healthful periodization is a high level system that includes changing supplement consumption in view of preparing cycles, objectives, and execution requests. This approach perceives that the body's wholesome requirements change over time, contingent upon variables, for example, the power and volume of preparing, rivalry timetable, and recuperation stages. By decisively controlling macronutrient proportions, caloric admission, and timing, competitors can upgrade execution, support preparing variations, and oversee body structure really.

The idea of stomach wellbeing has acquired noticeable quality lately, and its pertinence stretches out to strength competitors. The gastrointestinal plot assumes a urgent part in supplement retention, resistant capability, and generally prosperity. Awkward nature in stomach microbiota, frequently affected by elements like eating routine, stress, and drugs, can influence absorption and supplement usage. Counting fiber-rich food varieties, probiotics, and prebiotics in the eating routine can add to a sound stomach microbiome, supporting ideal supplement retention and in general stomach related capability.

Exploring the complicated scene of sustenance for strength requires an individualized methodology that considers factors like age, orientation, body creation, preparing experience, and explicit objectives. Talking with an enlisted dietitian or nourishment master can give customized direction, guaranteeing that dietary procedures line up with individual necessities and inclinations. Occasional appraisals and acclimations to the sustenance plan might be important to oblige changes in preparing volume, force, and objectives.

7.1 The importance of a balanced and nutritious diet in achieving fitness goals

In the complex excursion towards accomplishing wellness objectives, the meaning of a fair and nutritious eating regimen couldn't possibly be more significant. Whether the goal is weight reduction, muscle gain, further developed perseverance, or in general prosperity, the fuel we give our bodies assumes a vital part in molding the results of our wellness tries. The transaction among nourishment and active work makes a unique relationship, where the right dietary decisions can streamline execution, improve recuperation, and add to the fulfillment of individual wellness desires.

At the center of any fruitful wellness venture lies the comprehension that the body capabilities as a perplexing framework, requiring a different exhibit of supplements to ideally perform. These supplements, arranged into macronutrients (sugars, proteins, and fats) and micronutrients (nutrients and minerals), act as the structure blocks for cell capability, energy creation, and the bunch physiological cycles that help a functioning way of life.

Starches, frequently defamed in specific eating regimen patterns, are a key energy source and a foundation of a reasonable eating regimen. They are the body's favored fuel for most exercises, especially during extreme focus works out. Consuming a satisfactory measure of sugars guarantees that the glycogen stores in muscles and the liver are recharged, giving a promptly accessible energy hotspot for actual effort. Entire grains, organic products, vegetables, and vegetables are magnificent wellsprings of perplexing sugars that proposition supported energy discharge, advancing perseverance and supporting generally speaking wellbeing.

Proteins, contained amino acids, are fundamental for muscle fix, development, and upkeep. With regards to wellness objectives, protein expects a focal job in the recuperation cycle after work out prompted muscle harm. People participated in strength preparing, perseverance exercises, or any type of actual activity benefit from an expanded protein admission to work with muscle protein combination and limit muscle protein breakdown. Wellsprings of great protein incorporate lean meats, poultry, fish, eggs, dairy items, and plant-based choices like beans and nuts.

While starches and proteins give energy and underlying scaffolding, dietary fats add to in general wellbeing and assume a part in different physiological capabilities. Solid fats, like those tracked down in avocados, nuts, seeds, and olive oil, are pivotal for supplement assimilation, chemical creation, and the upkeep of cell layers. Perceiving the significance of integrating fats into a reasonable eating routine is fundamental, scattering the legend that all fats are negative to wellbeing. Finding some kind of harmony between various sorts of fats and staying away from exorbitant utilization of immersed and trans fats is vital to receiving the rewards of dietary fat without compromising wellbeing.

Micronutrients, enveloping nutrients and minerals, are essential parts of a nutritious eating regimen that help a scope of physiological cycles. Every nutrient and mineral assumes a remarkable part in cell capability, resistant reaction, bone wellbeing, and different parts of prosperity. For instance, L-ascorbic acid adds to collagen union and invulnerable capability, while calcium and vitamin D are fundamental for bone wellbeing. An eating routine wealthy in natural products, vegetables, entire grains, and dairy or strengthened plant-based choices can supply the body with a range of micronutrients.

The idea of energy balance is a fundamental standard in the domain of sustenance and wellness. It spins around the balance between energy admission and energy use. To accomplish weight-related wellness objectives, people should comprehend and deal with their energy balance actually.

A caloric excess, where admission surpasses use, is helpful for muscle gain, while a calorie deficiency, where consumption surpasses admission, is much of the time sought after for weight reduction. Finding some kind of harmony and taking into account the nature of calories consumed is significant for accomplishing and keeping a solid body organization.

Hydration, frequently ignored in conversations about nourishment and wellness, is a basic part of in general wellbeing and execution. Water is fundamental for various physiological cycles, including temperature guideline, assimilation, and supplement transport. Lack of hydration can disable activity execution, thwart recuperation, and even lead to antagonistic wellbeing impacts. Competitors and wellness lovers should focus on their liquid admission, particularly during serious instructional courses or exercises that incite huge perspiration misfortune. Electrolytes, which incorporate minerals like sodium, potassium, and magnesium, assume a part in liquid equilibrium and ought to be recharged when essential.

Understanding the planning of supplement admission is a nuanced part of sustenance that can fundamentally influence wellness results. The idea of supplement timing rotates around decisively consuming supplements at explicit times to streamline execution, recuperation, and transformations to work out. Pre-exercise nourishment plans to give the energy expected to the impending action, accentuating the significance of sugars for fuel. Post-exercise sustenance, normally alluded to as the "anabolic window," centers around renewing glycogen stores and supporting muscle protein blend with a mix of starches and protein. While supplement timing can upgrade execution for certain people, the general conveyance of macronutrients over the course of the day stays a basic thought.

The mental elements of nourishment and their effect on accomplishing wellness objectives ought to be considered carefully. The connection among food and feelings, normally known as profound eating, can impact dietary decisions and, thus, influence wellness results. Stress, tension, and other close to home variables can prompt undesirable eating ways of behaving, influencing both the quality and amount of food ate. Developing a positive outlook towards food, rehearsing careful eating, and looking for help when required can add to a better relationship with nourishment and, thusly, wellness achievement.

The advancing field of customized sustenance perceives that people answer distinctively to different dietary methodologies in view of variables like hereditary qualities, metabolic rate, and way of life. Fitting healthful systems to individual requirements and inclinations upgrades adherence and adequacy. Talking with an enlisted dietitian or sustenance expert can give customized direction, assisting people with exploring the intricate scene of nourishment and pursue informed decisions that line up with their interesting conditions and objectives.

Supplements, while not a substitute for a balanced eating routine, can offer designated help in specific circumstances. Competitors with explicit supplement inadequacies, those following prohibitive weight control plans, or people with expanded supplement necessities might profit from supplements.

Regularly involved supplements in the wellness domain incorporate multivitamins, omega-3 unsaturated fats, vitamin D, and protein powders. In any case, it is pivotal to move toward supplementation with alert, guaranteeing that it supplements as opposed to replaces a supplement thick eating routine.

Chasing wellness objectives, rest is a habitually disregarded however essential part of the recuperation interaction. Rest assumes a vital part in muscle fix, chemical guideline, and in general prosperity. Unfortunate rest quality or deficient rest can debilitate practice execution, thwart recuperation, and increment the gamble of injury. Laying out solid rest propensities, establishing a favorable rest climate, and focusing on sufficient rest add to in general wellness achievement.

The social part of sustenance adds one more layer of intricacy to the quest for wellness objectives. Group environments, social impacts, and friend elements can shape dietary decisions and effect adherence to nourishing plans. Exploring social circumstances, pursuing informed decisions in different conditions, and finding a harmony between friendly perspectives and individual objectives are fundamental contemplations in the excursion towards accomplishing and keeping up with wellness.

7.2 Tailoring nutrition to support muscle growth and recovery

Chasing ideal muscle development and recuperation, the job of nourishment arises as a basic component that can fundamentally impact results. Whether you are an enthusiastic rec center participant expecting to construct fit bulk or a competitor trying to improve execution, understanding how to fit your nourishment to help these objectives is principal. This includes a nuanced approach that considers macronutrient dispersion, supplement timing, hydration, and the coordination of enhancements to establish a synergistic climate helpful for muscle development and compelling recuperation.

Vital to the idea of muscle development is the significance of protein, a macronutrient prestigious for its job in muscle fix and union. Proteins are made out of amino acids, frequently alluded to as the structure blocks of muscle tissue. At the point when participated in obstruction preparing or different types of difficult active work, the muscles experience microtears that require fix. Satisfactory protein consumption gives the fundamental amino acids expected for this maintenance interaction, advancing muscle development and forestalling exorbitant breakdown.

The ideal protein admission for muscle development can shift in light of individual factors, for example, body weight, action level, and preparing power. As an overall rule, competitors and people zeroed in on muscle development frequently hold back nothing admission going from 1.6 to 2.2 grams of protein per kilogram of body weight. In any case, individual reactions might fluctuate, and it is prudent to calibrate protein admission in view of individual objectives, inclinations, and reaction to preparing.

Wellsprings of great protein incorporate lean meats, poultry, fish, eggs, dairy items, and plant-based choices like vegetables, tofu, and quinoa. The consolidation of an assortment of protein sources guarantees a different amino corrosive profile as well as gives fundamental nutrients and minerals that add to by and large wellbeing.

Past complete protein consumption, the dissemination of protein over the course of the day assumes a vital part in boosting muscle protein union. Research recommends that spreading protein consumption uniformly across dinners, incorporating a protein source in each, can upgrade the body's capacity to construct and fix muscle. This differences with the conventional spotlight on consuming a lot of protein in a solitary post-exercise feast, showing the significance of steady protein dissemination for supported muscle development.

Notwithstanding protein, carbs are essential to muscle development, filling in as a key energy source during exercises and recharging glycogen stores post-work out. Carbs give the energy expected to extreme focus instructional meetings, forestalling untimely exhaustion and permitting people to stretch their boundaries during obstruction preparing. Post-work out, consuming starches recharges glycogen stores, supporting recuperation and setting up the body for ensuing meetings.

The idea of sugar periodization includes changing starch admission in view of preparing force and volume. On days with additional requesting exercises, a higher starch admission might be justified to satisfy expanded energy needs. On the other hand, on rest days or during times of lower movement, a moderate starch admission can in any case give energy while forestalling pointless caloric excess.

Complex carbs from entire grains, organic products, vegetables, and vegetables are ideal over straightforward sugars because of their more slow assimilation and supported energy discharge. This lines up with supporting energy levels all through the whole exercise as opposed to giving a speedy spike followed by an accident. Offsetting sugar consumption with fiber-rich sources further adds to by and large stomach related wellbeing and gives a consistent arrival of energy.

While protein and carbs become the overwhelming focus in muscle development nourishment, dietary fats likewise assume a strong part. Sound fats add to chemical creation, including chemicals like testosterone that are associated with muscle development. Moreover, fats help in the retention of fat-solvent nutrients (A, D, E, and K) that are fundamental for different physiological cycles.

Counting wellsprings of sound fats, like avocados, nuts, seeds, and olive oil, in the eating regimen gives a balanced way to deal with macronutrient consumption. Finding some kind of harmony between various sorts of fats, underlining monounsaturated and polyunsaturated fats while directing soaked fat admission, is vital for generally wellbeing.

The objective isn't to stay away from fats yet to consolidate them wisely as a component of a decent eating regimen that supports muscle development and by and large prosperity.

Hydration is a key part of both activity execution and recuperation, making it a fundamental thought with regards to muscle development. Water is engaged with various physiological cycles, including supplement transport, temperature guideline, and waste end. Drying out can disable activity execution, impede recuperation, and compromise in general wellbeing.

The significance of hydration turns out to be especially articulated during opposition preparing and different types of active work that incite perspiring. Satisfactory liquid admission keeps up with electrolyte balance, forestalling parchedness related entanglements, for example, muscle issues and weakness. Electrolytes, including sodium, potassium, and magnesium, assume a vital part in muscle capability and ought to be recharged, particularly after serious instructional meetings.

Supplement timing, frequently examined with regards to pre-and post-exercise sustenance, is an essential methodology that can enhance muscle development and recuperation. Pre-exercise nourishment centers around giving the fundamental energy to the impending instructional meeting, guaranteeing that the body has the fuel expected for ideal execution. A decent mix of starches and a moderate measure of protein is frequently suggested for pre-exercise dinners.

Post-exercise nourishment, regularly alluded to as the "anabolic window," is a basic period for recharging glycogen stores and starting muscle protein blend. Consuming a mix of quick processing sugars and excellent protein inside the initial not many hours after practice is accepted to boost these cycles. This healthful technique expects to gain by the elevated responsiveness of muscle cells to supplements during this time, advancing proficient recuperation and muscle development.

While the idea of the anabolic window has been broadly examined, ongoing exploration recommends that the general circulation of supplements over the course of the day might be a higher priority than the quick post-practice time frame. Guaranteeing that dinners are even and contain a sufficient measure of protein and sugars can uphold muscle protein blend and glycogen renewal, regardless of whether consumed past the apparent anabolic window.

Enhancements can be significant devices chasing muscle development, yet they ought to supplement a balanced eating routine instead of supplant it. Creatine monohydrate stands apart as one of the most explored and powerful enhancements for muscle development. It upgrades strength and power, increments lean weight, and adds to further developed practice execution. Fanned chain amino acids (BCAAs), especially leucine, assume a part in animating muscle protein blend and diminishing muscle protein breakdown.

While these enhancements can offer advantages, it is vital to move toward supplementation with an educated viewpoint, taking into account individual necessities, objectives, and likely associations.

The idea of caloric excess is frequently connected with muscle development, as it gives the extra energy expected to the cycles of muscle fix, recuperation, and development. A caloric excess happens when energy consumption surpasses use, bringing about an overflow of calories that can be utilized for building muscle. While this approach is successful for some people trying to acquire lean mass, the size of the excess and the pace of weight gain ought to be painstakingly figured out how to keep away from extreme fat aggregation.

On the other hand, a calorie deficiency, where energy consumption surpasses admission, is generally utilized for those looking for fat misfortune while meaning to protect bulk. This requires a cautious equilibrium to guarantee that the shortage is adequate for fat misfortune without compromising muscle development and recuperation. Adjusting macronutrient conveyance and generally speaking supplement thickness becomes urgent in this situation to meet protein and energy needs successfully.

Grasping individual contrasts in metabolic rate, hereditary qualities, and preparing reaction is fundamental while fitting sustenance for muscle development. A few people might answer all the more well to sequential sugar consumption, while others might flourish with various protein levels. Checking progress, changing dietary techniques in view of criticism from the body, and perceiving the requirement for occasional evaluations are fundamental parts of a customized way to deal with nourishment.

All in all, fitting sustenance to help muscle development and recuperation requires a thorough comprehension of the transaction between macronutrients, micronutrients, hydration, and timing. Underscoring a protein-rich eating regimen to help muscle fix, consolidating carbs decisively to fuel exercises and renew glycogen stores, incorporating sound fats for by and large prosperity, and focusing on hydration add to a powerful wholesome structure.

Supplement timing, while once centered around thin windows around exercises, is advancing to stress predictable supplement circulation over the course of the day. The significance of enhancements, like creatine and BCAAs, can be perceived inside the setting of a balanced eating routine. Caloric contemplations, whether as an excess for muscle development or a shortage for fat misfortune, should be drawn nearer with a nuanced viewpoint that thinks about individual objectives and reactions.

7.3 Dispelling common myths about diet and fitness

In the tremendous scene of diet and wellness, a plenty of legends and confusions have multiplied throughout the long term, frequently obfuscating the way to informed navigation and fruitful wellbeing results. These legends, energized by falsehood, patterns, and recounted proof, can add to disarray and disappointment among people endeavoring to make positive way of life changes. To prepare for proof based rehearses and advance a sensible comprehension of diet and wellness, dissipating a portion of these normal misconceptions is fundamental.

Fantasy 1: Carbs Are the Adversary of Weight reduction

One winning fantasy in the domain of eating less junk food is the attack of sugars as the essential guilty party behind weight gain and obstruction to weight reduction. Starches are, as a matter of fact, a critical macronutrient that furnishes the body with energy, especially during extreme focus proactive tasks. The critical lies in recognizing various sorts of carbs.

Entire grains, natural products, vegetables, and vegetables are instances of complicated carbs that offer fundamental supplements, fiber, and supported energy discharge. Then again, refined carbs found in sweet bites and handled food sources can add to overabundance calorie utilization and frustrate weight reduction endeavors. The defamation of all starches misrepresents the dietary scene and ignores the significance of picking supplement thick sources inside this macronutrient class.

Fantasy 2: Eating Fat Makes You Fat

The thought that consuming dietary fat prompts weight gain has been a persevering fantasy. While the facts really confirm that dietary fat is calorie-thick, giving a larger number of calories per gram than starches or proteins, the connection between fat admission and muscle to fat ratio is more nuanced. Sound fats, like those tracked down in avocados, nuts, seeds, and olive oil, assume fundamental parts in chemical creation, supplement retention, and in general wellbeing.

It is vital to recognize solid fats and trans fats or over the top soaked fats, which might add to medical problems when consumed in huge amounts. A decent eating regimen that incorporates moderate measures of sound fats isn't just viable with weight the executives yet in addition upholds different physiological capabilities inside the body.

Legend 3: Cardio Is the Best way to Get in shape

Cardiovascular activity, usually known as cardio, has for some time been related with weight reduction, and keeping in mind that it is without a doubt useful for consuming calories and working on cardiovascular wellbeing, it isn't the selective answer for weight the executives. Opposition preparing, like weightlifting, is similarly significant in advancing weight reduction and generally speaking wellbeing.

Obstruction preparing fabricates fit bulk, which, thus, supports the body's basal metabolic rate. This implies that even very still, people with more muscle consume more calories. A balanced wellness schedule that incorporates both cardiovascular and obstruction activities can be more successful in accomplishing weight reduction objectives than depending exclusively on cardio.

Fantasy 4: Skipping Feasts Speeds up Weight reduction

The possibility that skipping feasts, especially breakfast, speeds up weight reduction is a typical confusion. While discontinuous fasting and dinner timing procedures can be viable for certain people, skipping feasts as a general way to deal with weight reduction can make unfavorable impacts. Denying the group of customary feasts can prompt expanded hunger, gorging during resulting dinners, and possibly a decline in digestion.

In addition, breakfast, frequently hailed as the main feast of the day, gives fundamental supplements and energy to launch the day. Skipping it might bring about diminished mental capability, lower energy levels, and debilitated actual execution. A more practical way to deal with weight reduction includes pursuing nutritious food decisions and embracing a reasonable eating design.

Fantasy 5: Spot Decrease Is Conceivable

The longing to target fat misfortune in unambiguous region of the body, known as spot decrease, is a tireless fantasy. Performing vast redundancies of activities focusing on a specific body part, for example, crunches for the stomach region, doesn't ensure limited fat misfortune. The body will in general lose fat efficiently, affected by elements like hereditary qualities, chemicals, and by and large calorie balance.

Participating in a complete wellness schedule that consolidates cardiovascular activity, opposition preparing, and a reasonable eating routine is more successful for by and large fat misfortune. As the body sheds fat, it does as such in still up in the air by hereditary factors as opposed to the particular muscles designated during exercise.

Legend 6: Eating Late Around evening time Causes Weight Gain

The conviction that eating late around evening time consequently prompts weight gain is a fantasy that misrepresents the complicated connection between dinner timing and body weight. Weight gain is fundamentally affected by the all out number of calories consumed over the course of the day and the harmony between energy admission and consumption.

Late-evening eating itself doesn't innately add to weight gain; it is the general quality and amount of food devoured that matter. If late-evening nibbling includes supplement thick, segment controlled decisions, it is probably not going to prompt weight gain. Notwithstanding, thoughtless utilization of unhealthy, sweet, or handled tidbits can add to an overabundance of calories, influencing weight the executives.

Fantasy 7: All Calories Are Made Equivalent

The possibility that all calories are made equivalent distorts the healthful intricacy of various food sources. While the facts really confirm that weight the board includes the harmony between calories consumed and calories consumed, the wellspring of those calories matters for in general wellbeing. The healthy benefit of food sources, including the presence of fundamental nutrients, minerals, and macronutrients, adds to their effect on the body.

For example, 100 calories from a sweet refreshment don't have similar dietary benefit as 100 calories from a serving of vegetables. The previous gives void calories without fundamental supplements, while the last option offers fiber, nutrients, and minerals that help generally wellbeing. An emphasis on the nature of calories, as opposed to exclusively the amount, is fundamental for a balanced and wellbeing advancing eating regimen.

Legend 8: You Can Out-Exercise a Horrible eating routine

The conviction that thorough activity can make up for a horrible eating routine is a typical misguided judgment that can impede people from arriving at their wellbeing and wellness objectives. While practice is a pivotal part of a solid way of life, it can't totally counterbalance the adverse consequences of an imbalanced or unfortunate eating regimen. Sustenance plays a central job in supporting generally speaking wellbeing, weight the board, and wellness results.

A balanced methodology that joins ordinary active work with a reasonable and nutritious eating regimen is the best technique for accomplishing and keeping up with ideal wellbeing. Depending exclusively on exercise to balance unfortunate dietary decisions might prompt poor outcomes and expanded hazard of medical problems.

Legend 9: Consuming less calories Ought to Be Extraordinary to Be Viable

Outrageous and prohibitive eating regimens, frequently encouraging quick weight reduction, are habitually connected with wellbeing and wellness patterns. Notwithstanding, these methodologies are many times impractical in the long haul and can antagonistically affect both physical and mental prosperity. While uncommon eating regimens might prompt beginning weight reduction, they are commonly difficult to keep up with, bringing about a pattern of weight recapture.

A more compelling and supportable methodology includes making steady, practical changes to dietary propensities. Embracing a decent and supplement thick eating design, alongside integrating normal actual work, cultivates long haul achievement and supports generally speaking wellbeing.

Fantasy 10: Enhancements Can Supplant a Solid Eating routine

The conviction that enhancements can substitute the requirement for a sound and adjusted diet is a misinterpretation that can have impeding results. While enhancements can assume an important part in tending to explicit supplement lacks or supporting specific wellbeing objectives, they are not a substitute for a balanced eating routine.

Entire food varieties give a blend of nutrients, minerals, fiber, and other useful mixtures that work synergistically to advance wellbeing. Depending entirely on enhancements might bring about passing up the assorted exhibit of supplements and phytochemicals tracked down in entire food varieties. It is prudent to see supplements as supplements to a nutritious eating routine instead of swaps for the expansive range of supplements given by entire, natural food varieties.

In the consistently developing scene of wellbeing and health, legends encompassing eating routine and wellness have flourished, frequently engendered by confusions, obsolete data, and a craving for handy solutions. These fantasies can lead people down off track ways, preventing their advancement and subverting their endeavors to accomplish ideal wellbeing. Dissipating these legends is urgent for cultivating a more exact and informed way to deal with diet and wellness, engaging people to settle on decisions that line up with their objectives and add to long haul prosperity.

Legend 1: Carbs are the Adversary of Weight reduction

One unavoidable fantasy that has persevered for a really long time is the criticism of sugars as the essential foe of weight reduction. While the facts really confirm that refined carbs found in sweet tidbits and handled food varieties can add to overabundance calorie utilization and obstruct weight reduction endeavors, the slander of all carbs misrepresents the dietary scene.

Sugars are a significant macronutrient that gives the body energy, especially during extreme focus proactive tasks. Entire grains, natural products, vegetables, and vegetables are instances of intricate sugars that offer fundamental supplements, fiber, and supported energy discharge. A decent way to deal with starches includes picking supplement thick sources and perceiving their significance in supporting in general wellbeing and actual execution.

Fantasy 2: Eating Fat Makes You Fat

The thought that consuming dietary fat leads straightforwardly to weight gain has been a persevering legend. While it is actually the case that dietary fat is more calorie-thick than carbs or proteins, the connection between fat admission and muscle versus fat is more nuanced. Solid fats, tracked down in avocados, nuts, seeds, and olive oil, assume fundamental parts in chemical creation, supplement assimilation, and by and large wellbeing.

Adjusted consumes less calories that incorporate moderate measures of solid fats are viable with weight the executives as well as help different physiological capabilities inside the body. It is urgent to recognize solid fats and trans fats or exorbitant soaked fats, perceiving that consolidating the right sorts of fats can add to generally prosperity.

Fantasy 3: Cardio is the Best way to Get thinner

While cardiovascular activity, regularly known as cardio, is helpful for consuming calories and working on cardiovascular wellbeing, the fantasy that it is the best way to get thinner distorts the intricacies of wellness. Obstruction preparing, like weightlifting, is similarly significant in advancing weight reduction and by and large wellbeing.

Obstruction preparing fabricates fit bulk, which supports the body's basal metabolic rate. This implies that people with more muscle consume more calories even very still. An exhaustive wellness schedule that incorporates both cardiovascular and opposition practices is more compelling for accomplishing weight reduction objectives than depending exclusively on cardio.

Legend 4: Skipping Feasts Speeds up Weight reduction

The misguided judgment that skipping feasts, especially breakfast, speeds up weight reduction has been sustained by different eating routine patterns. Notwithstanding, denying the group of customary dinners can prompt expanded hunger, gorging during ensuing feasts, and possibly a reduction in digestion.

Skipping feasts doesn't ensure weight reduction; it can upset the body's energy equilibrium and lead to irregular characteristics in supplement consumption. Breakfast, frequently hailed as the main dinner of the day, gives fundamental supplements and energy to launch the day. A more supportable way to deal with weight reduction includes pursuing nutritious food decisions and embracing a decent eating design.

Fantasy 5: Spot Decrease Is Conceivable

The longing to target fat misfortune in unambiguous region of the body, known as spot decrease, is a relentless legend that has deluded numerous people. Performing practices focusing on a specific body part, for example, crunches for the stomach region, doesn't ensure restricted fat misfortune. The body will in general lose fat efficiently, affected by elements like hereditary qualities, chemicals, and by and large calorie balance.

Taking part in a complete wellness schedule that consolidates cardiovascular activity, obstruction preparing, and a fair eating regimen is more compelling for in general fat misfortune. As the body sheds fat, it does as such in not entirely settled by hereditary factors as opposed to the particular muscles focused on during exercise.

Legend 6: Eating Late Around evening time Causes Weight Gain

The conviction that eating late around evening time consequently prompts weight gain misrepresents the connection between dinner timing and body weight. Weight gain is essentially impacted by the absolute number of calories consumed over the course of the day and the harmony between energy admission and consumption.

Late-evening eating itself doesn't intrinsically add to weight gain; it is the general quality and amount of food ate that matter. In the event that late-evening eating includes supplement thick, segment controlled decisions, it is probably not going to prompt weight gain. Be that as it may, careless utilization of fatty, sweet, or handled bites can add to an overabundance of calories, influencing weight the executives.

Fantasy 7: All Calories Are Made Equivalent

The idea that all calories are made equivalent distorts the dietary intricacy of various food sources. While weight the executives includes the harmony between calories consumed and calories consumed, the wellspring of those calories matters for in general wellbeing. The dietary benefit of food sources, including the presence of fundamental nutrients, minerals, and macronutrients, adds to their effect on the body.

For example, 100 calories from a sweet drink don't have similar healthy benefit as 100 calories from a serving of vegetables. The previous gives void calories absent any and all fundamental supplements, while the last option offers fiber, nutrients, and minerals that help in general wellbeing. Zeroing in on the nature of calories, as opposed to exclusively the amount, is fundamental for a balanced and wellbeing advancing eating regimen.

Fantasy 8: You Can Out-Exercise a Terrible eating routine

The conviction that thorough activity can make up for a terrible eating routine is a typical misguided judgment that can frustrate people from arriving at their wellbeing and wellness objectives. While practice is an essential part of a sound way of life, it can't completely balance the adverse consequences of an imbalanced or unfortunate eating routine. Sustenance plays a fundamental job in supporting generally speaking wellbeing, weight the board, and wellness results.

A balanced methodology that consolidates ordinary active work with a fair and nutritious eating regimen is the best technique for accomplishing and keeping up with ideal wellbeing. Depending entirely on exercise to neutralize unfortunate dietary decisions might prompt poor outcomes and expanded chance of medical problems.

Legend 9: Slimming down Ought to Be Radical to Be Compelling

Outrageous and prohibitive eating regimens, frequently encouraging fast weight reduction, are as often as possible related with wellbeing and wellness patterns. Be that as it may, these methodologies are much of the time impractical in the long haul and can antagonistically affect both physical and mental prosperity. While exceptional eating regimens might prompt starting weight reduction, they are normally difficult to keep up with, bringing about a pattern of weight recapture.

A more compelling and practical methodology includes making steady, reasonable changes to dietary propensities. Taking on a fair and supplement thick eating design, alongside integrating standard actual work, encourages long haul achievement and supports generally speaking wellbeing.

Legend 10: Enhancements Can Supplant a Solid Eating regimen

The conviction that enhancements can substitute the requirement for a sound and adjusted diet is a misguided judgment that can have hindering outcomes. While enhancements can assume an important part in tending to explicit supplement lacks or supporting specific wellbeing objectives, they are not a substitute for a balanced eating routine.

Entire food varieties give a mix of nutrients, minerals, fiber, and other helpful mixtures that work synergistically to advance wellbeing. Depending entirely on enhancements might bring about passing up the different exhibit of supplements and phytochemicals tracked down in entire food sources. It is prudent to see supplements as supplements to a nutritious eating regimen instead of swaps for the expansive range of supplements given by entire, natural food varieties.

Chapter 8

The Crucible of Endurance

In the rambling scope of reality, where the reverberations of presence resound through the grandiose texture, there arises a cauldron — a field of unmatched perseverance. Inside this pot, the powers of life and fate merge, forming the actual pith of the real world. It is a domain where the guts of creatures is tried, their flexibility inspected, and the flares of their spirits tempered. This cauldron isn't limited by the laws of material science or the imperatives of mortal discernment; it rises above the limits of the known and wanders into the unknown regions of the mystical.

In this pot of perseverance, substances from different domains wind up weaved in a vast dance. The dance isn't one of class and effortlessness, yet rather a wild tornado of difficulties and preliminaries. A dance requests faithful purpose, an unflinching obligation to navigate the tricky way spread out by the grandiose weaver. The members in this vast artful dance are not simple humans; they are creatures of ethereal importance, each conveying the heaviness of their own predetermination.

As the pot unfurls, the embroidered artwork of presence starts to unwind, uncovering strings of interconnectedness that tight spot the members inseparably. From the divine creatures that cross the astral planes to the natives of failed to remember domains, all are brought into the cauldron's gravitational draw. There can be no way out from its supreme impact, and as the members face the difficulties laid before them, they become keenly conscious about the pot's extraordinary power.

The main test appears as a maze of time, a labyrinth that exciting bends in the road, testing the actual texture of transient discernment. The people who enter this maze wind up exploring through ages and times, encountering the ascent and fall of developments in a split second. The maze is certainly not a simple significant hardship however a showdown with the transient idea of the real world. Time becomes both a partner and an enemy, an instrument of creation and obliteration.

In the midst of the transient maze, the members experience reverberations of their past and brief looks at their future. The limits between what was, what, and will be obscure, driving them to go up against the certainty of progress. Some backlash in dread, unfit to accommodate the fleetingness of their reality, while others embrace the transition, understanding that perseverance isn't simply about enduring the progression of time yet it its extraordinary potential to embrace.

As the members rise out of the transient maze, they end up in an immense enormous spread — an astral combat zone where the powers of request and disarray conflict in an ensemble of heavenly fighting. Here, perseverance takes on another importance, as the members are tried by the actual afflictions of fight as well as by the supernatural powers that oversee the universe. It is a skirmish of wills, a challenge of internal strength against the vast flows that look to disentangle the actual substance of being.

In the heavenly front line, unions are manufactured and sold out, predeterminations entwined and cut off. The members discover that perseverance isn't exclusively a singular pursuit yet an aggregate undertaking. The bonds they structure with their kindred voyagers become a wellspring of solidarity, a signal in the vast tumult. Together, they face the hardship of heavenly struggle, arising not solid yet changed, their perseverance demonstrated in the pot of grandiose fighting.

From the astral front line, the members are pushed into the profundities of an early stage domain — a domain immaculate by the hands of time, where the reverberations of creation resound through the actual texture of the real world. Here, the cauldron takes on an undefined shape, and the perseverance required isn't of the physical or mystical kind however a greatness of oneself. The members defy the early stage powers that birthed the universe, confronting the crude, unrestrained force of creation.

In the early stage domain, the members are deprived of their biases and deceptions. They face the void, the chasm from which everything come out. It is a frightening excursion into the chasm of self-disclosure, where the perseverance required is an acquiescence to the grandiose flows that course through the embroidery of presence. Some oppose the call of the chasm, sticking to the remainders of their inner self, while others plunge head-first into its profundities, embracing the disintegration of oneself.

As the members rise out of the early stage domain, they end up remaining at the edge of an enormous nexus — a union of real factors where the limits between universes disintegrate. It is a position of endless conceivable outcomes, where the decisions in the pot reverberate across the multiverse. Here, the perseverance required isn't just a trial of individual strength yet an acknowledgment of the interconnectedness, everything being equal.

In the enormous nexus, the members witness the heap ways that unfurl before them, each prompting unique fates. They understand that perseverance is certainly not a static quality yet a unique power that moves them forward on the consistently moving flows of presence. Decisions made in the pot resonate across the multiverse, forming the predeterminations of the members as well as the actual texture of reality itself.

As the members explore the infinite nexus, they experience reverberations of their past decisions and brief looks at the heap prospects that lie ahead. The heaviness of obligation pushes ahead upon them, as they understand that each choice, each activity, conveys outcomes that reverberation across the embroidery of presence. Perseverance turns into an ethical goal, a promise to explore the intricacies of the multiverse with shrewdness and uprightness.

In the last phase of the pot, the members end up remaining on the cliff of vast greatness — a greatness past the constraints of structure and personality. It is a domain where the limits among self and other, individual and group, obscure into a consistent embroidery of vast solidarity. Here, the perseverance required is an acquiescence to the unutterable, a converging with the infinite flows that weave the actual texture of the real world.

In the domain of grandiose greatness, the members defy a definitive truth — reality that presence is an unending turning into, a perpetual progression of vast energies that dance through the boundless field of the universe. The pot of perseverance, with every one of its hardships, was nevertheless a preface to this vast disclosure. The members comprehend that perseverance isn't a necessary evil yet an excursion into the vast profundities of the enormous secret.

As the members converge with the inestimable flows, they become vessels of greatness, courses through which the energies of the multiverse stream. They rise above the impediments of individual personality, becoming enormous creatures of boundless potential.

The cauldron of perseverance, with its transient mazes, astral war zones, early stage domains, and grandiose nexuses, filled in as the catalytic pot in which their spirits were refined and changed.

Thus, the pot of perseverance finishes its grandiose cycle, leaving afterward creatures of otherworldly insight and unlimited empathy. The woven artwork of presence, once frayed and worn out, is rewoven with strings of enormous solidarity and interconnectedness. The members, presently vast stewards of the multiverse, leave on another excursion — an excursion past the limits of existence, directed by the getting through light of infinite insight.

In the tremendous span of the universe, where the reverberations of the cauldron of perseverance wait, another part unfurls. It is a part composed not in words but rather in the grandiose energies that heartbeat through the embroidery of presence. The members, presently grandiose creatures of extraordinary mindfulness, proceed with their excursion into the unutterable secret of the multiverse, directed by the getting through fire of vast perseverance.

8.1 Exploring the role of endurance in physical fitness

Actual wellness, a multi-layered idea incorporating strength, endurance, adaptability, and generally prosperity, is a pursuit that draws in people across the globe. At the core of this try lies the vital component of perseverance — a quality that goes past simple actual limit and dives into the domains of mental flexibility, assurance, and the capacity to endure and defeat difficulties. In investigating the job of perseverance in actual wellness, we set out on an excursion that crosses the physiological, mental, and profound elements of the human experience.

Physiologically, perseverance is frequently connected with cardiovascular wellness — the body's capacity to support delayed times of actual work. This type of perseverance relies on the productive working of the cardiovascular framework, which incorporates the heart, veins, and lungs. High-impact perseverance, specifically, is a critical part of cardiovascular wellness, zeroing in on exercises that hoist the pulse and work on the body's ability to use oxygen. Participating in exercises like running, cycling, or swimming improves cardiovascular wellbeing as well as constructs an establishment for generally speaking perseverance.

As people stretch their actual boundaries in vigorous exercises, the body goes through variations to fulfill the expanded need for oxygen and energy. The heart turns out to be more proficient at siphoning blood, the lungs further develop their oxygen-trade limit, and the muscles adjust to successfully use energy more. These physiological variations add to improved perseverance, permitting people to take part in supported actual work without capitulating to weariness.

Past cardiovascular wellness, strong perseverance is one more essential part of actual wellness. Solid perseverance alludes to the capacity of muscles to apply force more than once over a lengthy period. This type of perseverance is crucial in different exercises, from lifting loads to performing bodyweight works out. People with great solid perseverance can take part in undertakings that require redundant muscle constrictions without encountering untimely muscle weakness.

The physiological premise of strong perseverance lies in the piece and capability of muscle strands. Muscles comprise of various fiber types, in particular sluggish jerk (Type I) and quick jerk (Type II) filaments. Slow-jerk filaments are more impervious to exhaustion and are appropriate for perseverance exercises, while quick jerk strands produce more power yet weariness all the more rapidly. Preparing pointed toward further developing solid perseverance includes focusing on both fiber types through a blend of opposition preparing and high-reiteration, low-obstruction works out.

As people progress in their actual wellness venture, the entwining of cardiovascular and strong perseverance becomes clear. Exercises that request an amicable mix of both, for example, high-intensity exercise or intense cardio exercise (HIIT), arise as compelling method for upgrading in general perseverance. These exercises challenge the cardiovascular framework while at the same time constructing solid perseverance, encouraging a complete way to deal with actual wellness.

In any case, the quest for perseverance in actual wellness reaches out past the limits of physiological variations. It reaches out into the domain of mental versatility and mental determination. Perseverance isn't simply a proportion of actual endurance yet an impression of one's ability to conquer mental boundaries, push through uneasiness, and continue even with difficulty.

In the mental aspect, perseverance appears as the capacity to keep up with concentration and inspiration during delayed actual work. Marathon runners, for example, frequently stress the significance of mental perseverance in finishing races. The tedium of a long distance race or a lengthy cycling venture requires a tough outlook — one that can explore the psychological exhaustion that goes with dreary, delayed effort.

The idea of the "unexpected surge of energy" epitomizes the mental part of perseverance. It alludes to a peculiarity where people, after a time of actual strain, experience a reestablished flood of energy and mental lucidity. This unexpected burst of energy isn't exclusively a result of physiological recuperation however a demonstration of the psychological determination that empowers people to push through the underlying inconvenience and track down reestablished strength.

Mental perseverance likewise assumes a significant part in sticking to long haul wellness objectives. The excursion to actual wellness is frequently described by pinnacles and valleys, progress and difficulties. Supporting a pledge to ordinary activity, sound sustenance, and way of life changes requires versatility despite challenges. People serious areas of strength for with perseverance can face the hardships of self-uncertainty, levels, and outer tensions, continuing in their quest for ideal wellbeing and wellness.

In addition, the job of perseverance reaches out into the profound domain, entwining with the feeling of achievement, fulfillment, and prosperity that people get from their actual wellness tries. The close to home prizes of perseverance are not bound to the snapshot of crossing an end goal or finishing a difficult exercise; they penetrate the texture of day to day existence. The certainty acquired through beating actual difficulties swells into different parts of life, cultivating a positive mental self view and a feeling of strengthening.

In the scene of actual wellness, perseverance fills in as an impetus for self-awareness and self-disclosure. It changes the person from somebody who just takes part in actual work to somebody who embraces difficulties, invites uneasiness, and flourishes chasing after nonstop improvement. The perseverance developed in the exercise center, on the track, or in the studio turns into a representation for exploring the intricacies of life — a tough establishment whereupon people can construct a satisfying and lively presence.

Besides, the investigation of perseverance in actual wellness reaches out past the singular level to envelop the public and cultural aspects. From an aggregate perspective, the quest for perseverance turns into a common undertaking that rises above social, geological, and cultural limits. Occasions like long distance races, marathons, and other perseverance races draw members from different foundations, making a feeling of fellowship and mutual perspective.

These mutual pursuits celebrate individual accomplishments as well as feature the aggregate strength that emerges when a local area meets up to beat difficulties. The common experience of stretching actual boundaries, supporting each other through the afflictions of preparing, and celebrating shared achievements encourages a feeling of solidarity and interconnectedness. Perseverance, in this specific circumstance, turns into a binding together power that scaffolds holes and rises above contrasts, underscoring the general human limit with respect to determination and strength.

Besides, the cultural ramifications of perseverance in actual wellness are reflected in the advancement of wellbeing and prosperity on a more extensive scale. Social orders that focus on and support ordinary active work add to the general soundness of their populaces. The advantages reach out past individual prosperity to include diminished medical care costs, expanded efficiency, and a for the most part better and more lively society.

Government drives, local area programs, and instructive missions pointed toward advancing actual wellness and perseverance assume a urgent part in molding cultural standards and ways of behaving. By encouraging a culture that qualities and focuses on actual work, social orders can relieve the weight of inactive ways of life and persistent medical issue. The getting through obligation to general wellbeing and wellness turns into an interest in the prosperity and imperativeness of people in the future.

In the instructive circle, the job of perseverance in actual wellness becomes the dominant focal point. Actual instruction programs, sports exercises, and wellness educational plans add to the comprehensive improvement of understudies. Past the actual advantages, these projects impart values like discipline, collaboration, and steadiness — characteristics that stretch out past the games field and into different features of life.

The instructive scene turns into a rich ground for developing an age with major areas of strength for an in actual wellness and perseverance. The examples learned through participating in sports, defeating difficulties, and taking a stab at individual outmaneuvers become necessary parts of character improvement. The persevering through soul cultivated in the instructive setting turns into a deep rooted resource, molding people who approach life's difficulties with flexibility and assurance.

In the corporate world, the importance of perseverance in actual wellness finds articulation in wellbeing projects and drives pointed toward advancing worker wellbeing and efficiency. Managers perceive the positive effect of actually dynamic and sound representatives on in general work environment elements. Actual work out regimes add to worked on actual wellbeing as well as act as source for pressure alleviation and group building.

The work environment, frequently portrayed by requesting timetables and high-pressure conditions, turns into a territory where perseverance takes on new aspects. Representatives who keep up with actual wellness get through the afflictions of their expert obligations with more prominent flexibility. The capacity to explore pressure, keep up with center, and support energy levels turns into an important resource in the cutting edge work environment, adding to individual achievement and the general prosperity of the association.

In looking at the job of perseverance in actual wellness, it becomes clear that its impact reaches out a long ways past the bounds of individual work-out schedules or athletic pursuits. It pervades the physiological, mental, profound, public, and cultural components of human life. The quest for perseverance turns into a dynamic and interconnected venture that shapes people and networks.

8.2 Strategies for building cardiovascular stamina

Cardiovascular endurance, frequently alluded to as cardiovascular perseverance or vigorous wellness, is a critical part of generally wellness and wellbeing. It mirrors the productivity of the cardiovascular framework in conveying oxygen to the muscles and eliminating side-effects during supported active work.

Building cardiovascular endurance isn't just fundamental for competitors and wellness devotees yet in addition for people trying to further develop their general prosperity and decrease the gamble of cardiovascular sicknesses. In this investigation of techniques for building cardiovascular endurance, we dive into an extensive methodology that envelops different types of oxygen consuming activity, moderate preparation strategies, and way of life contemplations.

One of the crucial methodologies for building cardiovascular endurance is taking part in normal oxygen consuming activity. Oxygen consuming activities, otherwise called cardio works out, include constant and musical exercises that hoist the pulse and increment respiratory movement. These exercises invigorate the cardiovascular framework, advancing variations that upgrade perseverance over the long run. Normal high-impact practices incorporate running, running, strolling, swimming, cycling, and moving.

Vigorous activities can be sorted into two fundamental sorts: low-effect and high-influence. Low-influence works out, like strolling and swimming, are gentler on the joints and are appropriate for people with joint worries or those new to work out. High-influence works out, like running and bouncing, are more extreme and can assist with working on cardiovascular endurance at a quicker rate. The decision between low-effect and high-influence practices relies upon individual inclinations, wellness levels, and any previous medical issue.

Assortment in vigorous exercises is urgent to building balanced cardiovascular endurance. Broadly educating, which includes integrating a blend of various vigorous activities into a wellness schedule, helps target different muscle gatherings and forestalls repetitiveness. For instance, consolidating cycling with swimming or shifting back and forth among running and paddling can give an extensive cardiovascular exercise. This approach upgrades endurance as well as decreases the gamble of abuse wounds related with tedious developments.

Notwithstanding assortment, the guideline of moderate over-burden is major to building cardiovascular endurance. Moderate over-burden includes step by step expanding the force, term, or recurrence of activity to constantly challenge the cardiovascular framework and prompt transformations. This can be accomplished by continuously expanding the distance or speed of running, the obstruction on an exercise bike, or the term of a cardio exercise. A slow and deliberate methodology permits the body to adjust and improve without excessive pressure or chance of injury.

Stretch preparation is a strong system inside the domain of moderate over-burden for building cardiovascular endurance. This strategy includes switching back and forth between times of extreme focus exercise and times of lower-power or rest. Extreme focus stretches push the cardiovascular framework to work at greatest limit, advancing expanded oxygen usage and cardiovascular proficiency. For example, a novice could shift back and forth between one moment of energetic strolling and 30 seconds of running, progressively advancing to additional extraordinary stretches as endurance gets to the next level.

Intense cardio exercise (HIIT) is a particular type of span preparing that has acquired prominence for its time productivity and viability in building cardiovascular endurance. HIIT includes short eruptions of serious activity followed by brief reprieve periods or low-power exercises. The extreme focus sections hoist the pulse to approach greatest levels, while the rest time frames take into account halfway recuperation before the following burst. HIIT can be adjusted to different types of cardio, like running, cycling, or even bodyweight practices like burpees and hopping jacks.

While stretch preparation is valuable for building cardiovascular endurance, offsetting focused energy exercises with moderate and low-power activities is fundamental. Consolidating consistent state high-impact work out, where the pulse is raised yet supported at a steady level for a lengthy period, further develops perseverance and vigorous limit. A balanced preparation program could incorporate a blend of span preparing, consistent state cardio, and recuperation days to consider ideal variation and forestall burnout.

Notwithstanding organized vigorous activity, integrating ordinary exercises that elevate cardiovascular wellbeing adds to building endurance. Strolling or cycling for transportation, using the stairwell rather than the lift, and participating in sporting exercises, for example, climbing or playing sports all add to generally speaking cardiovascular wellness. These way of life changes give extra open doors to vigorous activity as well as advance a more dynamic and wellbeing cognizant everyday daily schedule.

Consistency is a vital component in building cardiovascular endurance. Standard vigorous activity, whether as organized exercises or regular exercises, makes a steady upgrade for cardiovascular variations. Laying out a daily practice and sticking to a normal activity plan assists the body with adapting to the requests of oxygen consuming action, bit by bit further developing endurance over the long run. Vital to find an equilibrium is practical and charming, as long haul consistency is more important than inconsistent extreme endeavors.

Sustenance assumes a crucial part in supporting cardiovascular endurance. Satisfactory filling previously, during, and after oxygen consuming activity is fundamental for ideal execution and recuperation. Sugars are the essential energy hotspot for high-impact exercises, and consuming complex carbs before an exercise gives a promptly accessible wellspring of energy. Hydration is similarly vital, as parchedness can fundamentally hinder cardiovascular capability and perseverance. Keeping up with electrolyte balance, particularly during longer or more extreme exercises, further backings cardiovascular wellbeing.

Broadly educating stretches out past vigorous activities to incorporate strength preparing as an integral technique for building cardiovascular endurance. Strength preparing works on strong productivity, diminishes the gamble of injury, and improves generally actual execution.

A solid outer muscle framework upholds cardiovascular exercises by giving a steady groundwork to development and decreasing the gamble of abuse wounds. Counting obstruction preparing in a complete work out schedule adds to the comprehensive improvement of cardiovascular endurance.

Rest and recuperation are fundamental parts of any compelling preparation program pointed toward building cardiovascular endurance. Satisfactory rest, legitimate sustenance, and planned rest days permit the body to fix and adjust to the requests of activity. Overtraining, described by unnecessary activity without adequate recuperation, can prompt weariness, diminished execution, and an expanded gamble of injury. Offsetting testing exercises with times of rest guarantees supported progress and long haul cardiovascular wellbeing.

Observing advancement and putting forth practical objectives are fundamental parts of building cardiovascular endurance. Following key measurements, for example, pulse, exercise span, distance covered, and saw effort gives important bits of knowledge into execution and improvement. Setting reachable present moment and long haul objectives, whether connected with expanding exercise power or taking part in unambiguous occasions, keeps up with inspiration and gives a feeling of achievement as endurance gets to the next level.

Innovation can be a significant partner in the journey to fabricate cardiovascular endurance. Wearable wellness trackers, pulse screens, and cell phone applications offer apparatuses for observing and examining exercise information. These gadgets can give continuous criticism on pulse zones, pace, and other pertinent measurements, assisting people with streamlining their preparation and make informed changes. Furthermore, the gamification of wellness through applications and online stages can add a component of tomfoolery and contest to cardiovascular exercises, upgrading inspiration.

Bunch wellness classes and social help contribute fundamentally to building cardiovascular endurance. Joining bunch exercises or classes adds a social part to practice as well as acquaints assortment and design with the wellness schedule. The aggregate energy and consolation from individual members can help inspiration and cultivate a feeling of responsibility. Whether partaking in a running club, cycling gathering, or dance class, the shared part of gathering wellness upgrades the general insight of building cardiovascular endurance.

Mind-body rehearses, for example, yoga and care reflection, supplement cardiovascular preparation by tending to the psychological and profound parts of wellness. Stress the board and mental flexibility are vital parts of getting through active work. Consolidating exercises that advance unwinding and mental concentration, like yoga or profound breathing activities, can upgrade generally prosperity and add to a positive outlook during cardiovascular exercises.

The climate where cardiovascular activity happens can influence the experience and adequacy of the exercise. Outside exercises, for example, running or cycling give openness to natural air, normal view, and differing landscape, adding a component of oddity and pleasure to the work-out daily practice. Also, openness to regular light and daylight upholds circadian rhythms and in general prosperity. Choosing different conditions for oxygen consuming activity can forestall repetitiveness and improve the general insight.

In synopsis, the methodologies for building cardiovascular endurance envelop a complex methodology that coordinates different types of oxygen consuming activity, moderate preparation techniques, way of life contemplations, and steady practices.

8.3 Cross-training and its benefits for overall fitness

Broadly educating, a flexible and comprehensive way to deal with wellness, has earned inescapable respect for its capacity to upgrade generally speaking actual well-being and prosperity. Dissimilar to conventional types of activity that emphasis on a particular sort of movement, broadly educating includes integrating different exercises and exercises into a thorough wellness schedule. This variety not just gives a balanced way to deal with functional preparing yet in addition offers a scope of advantages that reach out past the bounds of specific preparation. In this investigation of broadly educating and its advantages for by and large wellness, we dig into the different parts of this methodology, including further developed execution, decreased chance of injury, upgraded mental prosperity, and expanded inspiration.

One of the essential advantages of broadly educating lies in its ability to work on by and large actual execution. By participating in various exercises that target different muscle gatherings and energy frameworks, people can foster a more adjusted and flexible degree of wellness. For instance, consolidating cardiovascular activities like running or cycling with strength preparing, adaptability work, and exercises, for example, swimming or yoga makes a synergistic impact. This thorough methodology tends to numerous parts of actual wellness, prompting further developed perseverance, strength, adaptability, and coordination.

Cardiovascular wellness, a vital part of by and large wellbeing, is really tended to through broadly educating. Consolidating exercises that raise the pulse and challenge the cardiovascular framework, like running, cycling, swimming, or paddling, advances perseverance and heart wellbeing. By differentiating the kinds of cardiovascular activities, people forestall tedium as well as guarantee a more careful improvement of vigorous limit. This adaptability converts into further developed execution in different proactive tasks and everyday errands that require cardiovascular perseverance.

Strength preparing, one more fundamental part of broadly educating, adds to by and large wellness by developing solid fortitude and perseverance. Obstruction practices utilizing body weight, free loads, or machines target different muscle gatherings, improving generally outer muscle capability.

By integrating strength preparing into a broadly educating routine, people foster a strong and even body. This supports exercises that request strength as well as adds to further developed act, joint steadiness, and in general actual versatility.

Adaptability and versatility are in many cases neglected parts of wellness that assume a urgent part in by and large prosperity. Broadly educating, while including exercises like yoga or Pilates, advances adaptability by extending and protracting muscles. Further developed adaptability adds to upgraded joint scope of movement, diminished muscle firmness, and a diminished gamble of wounds connected with tight muscles. Also, exercises that accentuate adaptability upgrade body mindfulness and advance better stance, converting into worked on generally versatility and practical development.

Diminishing the gamble of injury is a conspicuous advantage of broadly educating. Specific preparation in a solitary movement, particularly when performed dully, can prompt abuse wounds and irregular characteristics in the outer muscle framework. Broadly educating mitigates this gamble by conveying the actual pressure across different exercises and muscle gatherings. For example, sprinters who integrate strength preparing, cycling, or swimming into their routine might encounter decreased influence on the joints and a lower hazard of running-related wounds. The fair methodology of broadly educating assists people with keeping a feasible and injury-safe wellness schedule.

One more benefit of broadly educating is its capacity to forestall exercise levels. At the point when people participate in a similar kind of activity over and over, the body adjusts, and the pace of progress may level. Broadly educating presents assortment and difficulties the body in various ways, forestalling variation and advancing consistent advancement. By routinely exchanging among exercises and consolidating new activities, people keep their exercises new and animating, prompting supported enhancements in wellness levels.

Mental prosperity is a significant part of generally speaking wellbeing, and broadly educating has been displayed to decidedly affect emotional well-being and mental capability. Actual work, as a general rule, is related with the arrival of endorphins, which are synapses that add to a feeling of prosperity and lessen pressure. Broadly educating, with its different exercises, permits people to pick exercises that they appreciate, encouraging an inspirational perspective towards work out. The assortment and curiosity related with broadly educating additionally add to mental excitement, forestalling fatigue and advancing supported inspiration.

Also, the social part of specific broadly educating exercises, for example, bunch classes or group activities, can improve mental prosperity. Social scenes give potential open doors to social collaboration, support, and a feeling of local area. The kinship and shared encounters in bunch exercises add to a positive and propelling climate. This social part can be especially advantageous for people who track down inspiration through association and shared objectives.

Broadly educating offers an important answer for people with time imperatives or the individuals who battle to stick to a solitary, dreary work-out daily practice. The adaptability of broadly educating permits people to modify their exercises in light of their timetable, inclinations, and accessible assets. Whether integrating speedy, stop and go aerobic exercise (HIIT) meetings, short strength exercises, or longer cardio exercises, people can fit their broadly educating routine to accommodate their way of life. This flexibility improves the probability of adherence to an ordinary work-out daily practice.

For people with explicit wellness objectives or those preparation for a specific game or occasion, broadly educating can be an essential supplement to their essential preparation. For instance, a marathon runner could consolidate strength preparing, cycling, or swimming to improve generally wellness without over-burdening the joints. Broadly educating permits people to address shortcomings, irregular characteristics, or explicit areas of progress, making a more complete and designated way to deal with preparing.

Moreover, broadly educating can be an important device for recovery and injury counteraction. People recuperating from wounds or with prior conditions can alter their work-out everyday practice to oblige their particular necessities. Low-influence exercises, like swimming or cycling, can be incorporated to give cardiovascular activity without putting exorbitant weight on harmed joints. Fortifying activities focusing on unambiguous muscle gatherings can help with recovery and forestall further wounds.

Broadly educating reaches out past the limits of customary exercise center exercises to incorporate open air exercises and sporting games. Exercises like climbing, kayaking, rock climbing, or playing group activities add to by and large wellness as well as give a feeling of experience and delight. The outside and sporting part of broadly educating adds a component of enjoyable to work out, advancing a positive relationship with active work and lessening the impression of exercises as a task.

In outline, broadly educating arises as a diverse way to deal with by and large wellness that offers a range of advantages. From further developed execution and decreased hazard of injury to upgraded mental prosperity and expanded inspiration, broadly educating addresses different parts of actual wellbeing and adds to an all encompassing way to deal with wellness. The flexibility and versatility of broadly educating make it open to people of various wellness levels, inclinations, and ways of life. By embracing a different scope of exercises, people can encounter the synergistic impacts of broadly educating, opening a way to supported wellbeing, prosperity, and wellness.

As people set out on their wellness process, the quest for generally wellbeing and prosperity turns into a main impetus. The idea of by and large wellness envelops an all encompassing way to deal with physical, mental, and profound prosperity.

It goes past the limited bounds of detached work-out schedules or explicit wellbeing objectives, expecting to develop an extensive condition of health. In this investigation of the advantages of generally speaking wellness, we dig into the interconnected parts of actual wellbeing, mental strength, close to home equilibrium, and the positive effect on day to day existence.

One of the basic advantages of generally wellness is the improvement of cardiovascular wellbeing. Ordinary active work, particularly vigorous activity, advances serious areas of strength for an effective cardiovascular framework. Exercises like running, cycling, swimming, and energetic strolling raise the pulse, working on the flow of blood and oxygen all through the body. This improves the soundness of the heart, lessens the gamble of cardiovascular illnesses, and adds to by and large cardiovascular wellness.

In addition, the beneficial outcomes of in general wellness reach out to weight the board and body organization. Taking part in a balanced wellness schedule that incorporates both cardiovascular activities and strength preparing upholds weight reduction or weight support objectives. Vigorous activities consume calories and add to fat misfortune, while strength preparing assembles slender bulk, which further lifts the digestion. The blend of these exercises encourages a solid body creation and supports economical weight the board.

Strength and strong perseverance are necessary parts of in general wellness. Strength preparing works out, whether utilizing body weight, free loads, or obstruction machines, add to the improvement of muscle strength. Strong perseverance, the capacity of muscles to perform dreary constrictions over a lengthy period, is additionally further developed through standard opposition preparing. Solid and strong muscles support everyday exercises as well as add to all the more likely stance, decreased chance of injury, and improved actual execution.

The advantages of generally speaking wellness reach out to bone wellbeing, a frequently neglected part of prosperity. Weight-bearing activities, like strolling, running, or opposition preparing, animate the bones and advance bone thickness. This is especially significant for forestalling osteoporosis and keeping up with skeletal wellbeing, particularly as people age. An extensive wellness schedule that incorporates exercises focusing on bone wellbeing adds to generally actual versatility and life span.

Adaptability and joint portability, frequently disregarded parts of wellness, are urgent for by and large prosperity. Exercises like yoga, Pilates, and dynamic extending advance adaptability and work on joint scope of movement. Improved adaptability adds to more readily act, decreases the gamble of wounds connected with muscle snugness, and supports generally joint wellbeing. The consideration of adaptability practices in a balanced wellness routine encourages a more adjusted and useful body.

Past the actual advantages, in general wellness significantly affects mental prosperity. Customary active work is related with the arrival of endorphins, synapses that go about as regular mind-set lifters and stress minimizers. The beneficial outcomes of activity on psychological well-being incorporate diminished side effects of nervousness and wretchedness, worked on mental capability, and improved generally speaking close to home prosperity. The psyche body association laid out through actual work adds to a stronger and positive mental state.

Mental capability and mind wellbeing are emphatically impacted by generally speaking wellness. Practice has been displayed to improve mental capacities, including memory, consideration, and leader capability. The expanded blood stream and oxygen conveyance to the mind during active work support the development of new neurons and the arrangement of brain associations. Standard activity is related with a decreased gamble old enough related mental deterioration and neurodegenerative circumstances, adding to generally mind wellbeing.

Rest quality and generally speaking energy levels are decidedly affected by customary active work. Taking part in moderate-force work out, for example, energetic strolling or cycling, has been displayed to further develop rest designs and advance better rest quality. Furthermore, generally wellness upholds the productive working of the body's energy frameworks, prompting expanded endurance and perseverance all through everyday exercises. The positive effect on rest and energy levels adds to a more dynamic and useful day to day routine.

The advantages of in general wellness stretch out to the resistant framework, upgrading the body's capacity to guard against diseases and contaminations. Standard activity has been related with a lift in resistant capability, including the creation of safe cells and antibodies. While extraordinary or delayed exercise may briefly smother the safe framework, moderate and reliable active work upholds insusceptible wellbeing. Generally speaking wellness, accomplished through a decent and economical work-out everyday practice, adds to a strong resistant framework.

Moreover, in general wellness emphatically impacts metabolic wellbeing, assuming a vital part in the counteraction and the executives of metabolic circumstances like diabetes. Ordinary activity further develops insulin awareness, permitting cells to all the more actually use glucose for energy. This, joined with the constructive outcomes on body creation and weight the executives, adds to generally speaking metabolic wellbeing. An extensive wellness schedule that incorporates both cardiovascular and strength preparing practices upholds ideal metabolic capability.

Social prosperity is a frequently neglected element of in general wellness. Taking part in bunch wellness classes, group activities, or open air exercises encourages social associations and a feeling of local area. The kinship and shared encounters in social scenes add to a positive and persuading climate.

The social part of in general wellness upgrades the satisfaction in practice as well as advances a steady organization, decreasing sensations of confinement and adding to by and large friendly prosperity.

The positive effect of generally speaking wellness on mental strength and stress the executives is especially critical. Practice goes about as a strong pressure reliever, assisting with reducing strain and further develop state of mind. The arrival of endorphins during active work adds to a characteristic decrease in pressure chemicals. Normal activity additionally gives an open door to care and unwinding, particularly in exercises like yoga or reflection, further supporting pressure decrease and in general mental strength.

With regards to in general wellness, the expression "practical wellness" has acquired conspicuousness. Practical wellness centers around practices that work on the body's capacity to effectively perform everyday exercises and developments. This approach stresses developments that impersonate genuine exercises, like bowing, lifting, bending, and coming to. Practical wellness upgrades actual execution in ordinary undertakings as well as lessens the gamble of wounds connected with ill-advised development designs.

Way of life contemplations, including nourishment and hydration, assume an essential part in generally speaking wellness. An even and nutritious eating routine backings energy levels, muscle recuperation, and generally speaking wellbeing. Sufficient hydration is fundamental for ideal physical processes and helps in the guideline of internal heat level during exercise. The reconciliation of solid dietary propensities into a general wellness plan upgrades the constructive outcomes of activity on actual wellbeing and prosperity.

One of the persevering through advantages of in general wellness is the advancement of life span and solid maturing. Ordinary actual work is related with an expanded life expectancy and a diminished gamble of ongoing illnesses related with maturing. The mix of cardiovascular wellness, strength preparing, adaptability activities, and in general wellbeing advancement adds to a more excellent of life as people age. Generally speaking wellness upholds the support of utilitarian freedom and a functioning way of life all through the maturing system.

Furthermore, the beneficial outcomes of in general wellness reach out to confidence and self-perception. Taking part in customary actual work and accomplishing wellness objectives add to a positive self-discernment. The feeling of achievement, further developed body structure, and upgraded actual capacities encourage a more good self-perception and fearlessness. Generally wellness, when drawn nearer with an emphasis on all encompassing prosperity, advances a sound connection with one's body and adds to a positive mental self portrait.

Chapter 9

Forged in Steel: Achieving Lasting Transformation

In the cauldron of life, where the flares of difficulty consume the most brilliant, and the sledge blows of challenge hit with unwavering power, people and social orders the same are manufactured in steel. Change, the speculative chemistry of progress, is an interaction that requests strength, fortitude, and a tenacious obligation to development. This excursion, set apart by preliminaries and wins, shapes the actual substance of our being, forming us into the designers of our fate.

At the core of enduring change lies the steadfast soul of assurance. It is the dauntless will to defy difficulties head-on, to explore the tricky flows of vulnerability, and to arise on the opposite side, more grounded and smarter. As we set out on the mission for persevering through change, we observe that the way isn't direct, yet rather a maze of self-revelation and development. Each diversion, every obstruction and leap forward, adds to the transformation of our personality.

One of the foundations of enduring change is mindfulness. To fashion oneself in steel, one must initially grasp the natural substance within reach. This contemplative excursion includes stripping back the layers of molding, going up against the shadows inside, and embracing the sum of one's presence. It is a course of recognizing qualities and shortcomings the same, and tolerating the obligation to shape one's fate with purposefulness.

Change, similar to steel, requires an intensity source. Misfortune, in its horde structures, fills in as the pot in which our backbone is tried. Whether it be private mishaps, proficient difficulties, or cultural disturbances, the intensity of affliction refines us, consuming with smoldering heat the pollutions of lack of concern and imparting inside us the flexibility expected to persevere. It is through confronting the cauldron that we become familiar with the genuine degree of our abilities and find repositories of solidarity we never knew existed.

As we explore the pot of life, the significance of persistence becomes obvious. The excursion towards enduring change isn't a run yet a long distance race, requesting supported exertion over the long run. Despite mishaps and disappointments, the strong soul continues on, gaining from the experience, adjusting, and pushing forward with unfaltering assurance. It is through constancy that the unrefined substance of potential is formed into the getting through substance of accomplishment.

A fundamental part of accomplishing enduring change is the development of a development outlook. A development outlook blossoms with difficulties, considers work to be a way to dominance, and perspectives misfortunes as any open doors for learning and improvement. Embracing a development mentality empowers people to rise above restrictions, get through deliberate hindrances, and ceaselessly develop towards their maximum capacity. The steel fashioned in the pot of a development mentality isn't weak yet adaptable, equipped for twisting without breaking.

In the journey for enduring change, the job of mentorship couldn't possibly be more significant. Similarly as a smithy directs the understudy in the sensitive craft of producing steel, tutors give significant direction, shrewdness, and backing on the excursion of individual and expert turn of events. The trade of information and experience among coach and mentee makes a cooperative energy that moves the course of change forward, cultivating a tradition of development that reaches out past individual lifetimes.

The force of local area and association arises as a focal subject in the story of enduring change. People are intrinsically friendly creatures, and the bonds we fashion with others act as an impetus for change. Whether as familial connections, kinships, or cooperative undertakings, the aggregate strength of a strong local area gives a repository of support, shared information, and shared assets. In the pot of local area, people track down comfort, motivation, and the aggregate will to get through the difficulties that change definitely involves.

Enduring change is certainly not a lone undertaking; it is a cooperative orchestra of shared goals and common help. As we explore the intricacies of life, the amicable transaction of different viewpoints enhances the woven artwork of our encounters. The manufacturing of enduring securities inside networks encourages a climate where people can gain from one another, challenge each other, and by and large lift the whole gathering towards more noteworthy levels of accomplishment.

The cauldron of change reaches out past the person to incorporate the cultural and authoritative domains. Similarly as people face difficulties and open doors for development, so too do networks, establishments, and social orders. The producing of steel for a bigger scope requests aggregate contemplation, versatile initiative, and a guarantee to values that endure everyday hardship. Cultural change, similar to the singular excursion, requires a harmony between saving the quintessence of personality and embracing the certainty of progress.

In the pot of cultural change, the job of administration arises as a basic component. Pioneers, whether in the general population or confidential area, bear the obligation of directing their associations through the violent waters of progress. The viability of administration in encouraging enduring change lies in its capacity to motivate, convey a convincing vision, and develop a culture of advancement and flexibility. Similarly as a gifted smithy shapes liquid metal with accuracy, viable pioneers form the aggregate predetermination of their associations.

A foundation of enduring change inside associations is the development of a culture of learning. In the consistently developing scene of the cutting edge world, associations should embrace a mentality that focuses on constant learning and transformation. The capacity to forget obsolete practices, gain new abilities, and encourage a culture of interest positions associations to flourish even with dynamic difficulties. The steel manufactured in the cauldron of a learning association isn't areas of strength for just likewise deft, fit for exploring the intricacies of a quickly evolving climate.

Cultural change is in many cases joined by the need for foundational change. Similarly as a smithy should reshape the shape to produce an alternate sort of sharp edge, social orders should reconsider and overhaul frameworks that never again serve the aggregate great. This cycle includes a basic assessment of strategies, foundations, and designs to guarantee they line up with the upsides of value, equity, and supportability. The steel produced in the cauldron of foundational change is one that embraces inclusivity, decency, and the prosperity of every one of its individuals.

In the excursion towards enduring cultural change, the job of training couldn't possibly be more significant. Schooling fills in as the cauldron in which the personalities of people in the future are formed and shaped.

An all encompassing school system grants information and abilities as well as ingrains values, decisive reasoning, and a feeling of obligation towards everyone's benefit. The steel fashioned through an extraordinary schooling is one that values long lasting learning, embraces variety, and adds to the improvement of society.

The cauldron of cultural change likewise requests a reexamination of monetary standards. As social orders advance, so too should the monetary frameworks that support them. The fashioning of an impartial and maintainable monetary model includes a shift towards mindful utilization, ecological stewardship, and the evenhanded dissemination of assets. The steel manufactured in the pot of a supportable economy is one that offsets thriving with ecological cognizance, guaranteeing the prosperity of current and people in the future.

Enduring change on a cultural scale requires a pledge to civil rights and correspondence. The pot of civil rights requests a resolute devotion to destroying foundational disparities, tending to verifiable treacheries, and making a general public where all people have equivalent chances to flourish. The steel manufactured in the cauldron of civil rights is one that champions variety, inclusivity, and the inborn worth of each and every person.

As we dig further into the complexities of enduring cultural change, the significance of natural stewardship becomes evident. The pot of ecological obligation requires a change in outlook towards maintainable practices, protection of regular assets, and an aggregate obligation to moderating the effect of environmental change. The steel manufactured in the pot of ecological stewardship is one that perceives the interconnectedness of every living being and the obligation to safeguard the planet for people in the future.

The excursion of enduring cultural change isn't without its difficulties. Protection from change, settled in power structures, and the idleness of laid out standards can go about as considerable snags. Notwithstanding, it is in the pot of affliction that the genuine strength of cultural change is uncovered. The aggregate will of a general public to face and defeat these difficulties is the power that tempers the steel of enduring change.

In the amazing embroidered artwork of mankind's set of experiences, instances of enduring cultural change proliferate. From developments upholding for social equality to the push for orientation uniformity, social orders have exhibited the ability to develop, adjust, and reclassify themselves in quest for an additional fair and even-handed world. The steel produced in the cauldron of cultural change fills in as a demonstration of the persevering through force of human organization and the ability to shape a superior future.

The story of enduring change stretches out past the individual and cultural domains to include the worldwide scene.

In a period portrayed by interconnectedness and relationship, the producing of a supportable and agreeable world requires cooperative endeavors on a worldwide scale. The cauldron of worldwide change requests participation, discretion, and a common obligation to tending to the squeezing difficulties that rise above borders.

One of the critical difficulties in the cauldron of worldwide change is the mission for harmony. In a world set apart by international pressures, equipped struggles, and the danger of atomic multiplication, the producing of worldwide harmony requires an aggregate will to focus on exchange, strategy, and compromise. The steel produced in the pot of worldwide harmony is one that esteems the holiness of human existence, regards the power of countries, and perceives the interconnectedness of the worldwide local area.

The cauldron of worldwide change additionally includes the basic of resolving squeezing worldwide issues, for example, environmental change, pandemics, and neediness. The fashioning of a feasible world requests cooperative endeavors to moderate the effect of environmental change, guarantee admittance to medical services for all, and kill destitution on a worldwide scale. The steel fashioned in the pot of worldwide manageability is one that focuses on the prosperity of the planet and its occupants over momentary additions.

The job of innovation in the cauldron of worldwide change can't be disregarded. During a time of fast mechanical progression, the manufacturing of an innovatively engaged world requires moral contemplations, dependable development, and a promise to bridling innovation for everyone's benefit. The steel fashioned in the pot of worldwide innovation is one that use development to address cultural difficulties, upgrade availability, and set out open doors for fair advancement.

Chasing enduring worldwide change, the significance of global participation becomes clear. The fashioning of collusions, the foundation of shared objectives, and the obligation to shared values are fundamental in exploring the intricacies of a globalized world. The steel fashioned in the pot of worldwide collaboration is one that rises above public limits, cultivating a feeling of shared liability regarding the prosperity of mankind in general.

As we examine the huge field of the pot of worldwide change, the job of people in the future arises as a point of convergence. The steel manufactured in the pot of worldwide change isn't just an impression of the present yet additionally a heritage for the people who will acquire the world. The obligation to pass on a world described by harmony, maintainability, and equity highlights the intergenerational idea of the extraordinary excursion.

All in all, the story of "Produced in Steel: Accomplishing Enduring Change" unfurls as an embroidery woven with strings of versatility, diligence, mindfulness, local area, authority, and cultural development. Whether at the individual, cultural, or worldwide level, the cauldron of change requests an aggregate obligation to development, versatility, and the getting through quest for a superior world.

As we explore the exciting bends in the road of life's pot, may we be propelled by the steel fashioned in the flames of change, exemplifying the strength, versatility, and getting through soul that describe enduring change.

9.1 Celebrating success stories of individuals who have transformed their bodies and lives

In the amazing embroidery of human encounters, accounts of individual change stand apart as guides of motivation. Among the horde stories that unfurl in the sections of our lives, those that middle around the noteworthy change of both body and soul reverberate profoundly. These examples of overcoming adversity act as demonstrations of the unbelievable limit with regards to change that dwells inside us, exhibiting the force of assurance, discipline, and flexibility.

At the core of these groundbreaking excursions lies the acknowledgment that change isn't only physical; a comprehensive transformation envelops the whole self. Whether driven by a longing for further developed wellbeing, expanded imperativeness, or a reestablished identity certainty, people set out on these excursions with a dream of a superior, more engaged rendition of themselves.

One of the significant components in these examples of overcoming adversity is the affirmation of the interconnectedness among physical and mental prosperity. The choice to leave on an extraordinary excursion frequently starts with a change in mentality — a pledge to focus on wellbeing and embrace the difficulties that accompany change. This psychological change makes way for the actual transformation that follows, making a cooperative energy between the brain and body.

The excursion toward changing one's body and life is diverse, incorporating different parts of way of life, sustenance, and wellness. Examples of overcoming adversity frequently feature the significance of embracing a decent and practical way to deal with these components. Instead of surrendering to prevailing fashion diets or outrageous activity regimens, people who effectively change their bodies focus on long haul wellbeing, embracing propensities that can be kept up with throughout a lifetime.

Nourishment, as a foundation of actual change, assumes a critical part in these examples of overcoming adversity. People frequently find the significant effect of sustaining their bodies with healthy, supplement thick food sources. The excursion includes a change in dietary decisions as well as a more profound comprehension of the body's nourishing requirements. These examples of overcoming adversity highlight the meaning of survey food as fuel as well as a wellspring of imperativeness and food for the body's perplexing frameworks.

Supplementing the dietary viewpoint is the obligation to normal active work. Fruitful changes frequently include the joining of work-out schedules custom fitted to individual objectives and inclinations.

From cardiovascular exercises that support perseverance to strength preparing that forms muscle, these examples of overcoming adversity exhibit the variety of wellness moves toward that can add to a changed physical make-up. Significantly, they underline the job of consistency, step by step developing fortitude and endurance over the long run.

Past the actual viewpoints, the festival of examples of overcoming adversity reaches out to the psychological and profound strength that people develop on their extraordinary excursions. These stories every now and again address the difficulties confronted — snapshots of self-uncertainty, mishaps, and the constancy expected to beat hindrances. The psychological guts exhibited in these accounts turns into a wellspring of motivation, empowering others to explore their own obstacles earnestly and elegance.

An ongoing idea in these examples of overcoming adversity is the acknowledgment that change is certainly not a direct way. It is set apart by pinnacles and valleys, progress and levels. The ability to embrace the excursion, gain from misfortunes, and continue even with difficulties separates the people who effectively change their bodies and lives. These accounts advise us that flexibility isn't the shortfall of misfortune however the capacity to rise more grounded after each fall.

Social help arises as a huge calculate the examples of overcoming adversity of body and life change. Whether through the consolation of companions, family, or local area, people track down strength in shared encounters. The festival of accomplishments turns into an aggregate undertaking, encouraging a feeling of association and having a place. Examples of overcoming adversity frequently feature the groundbreaking influence of a steady organization, showing that the excursion is more enhancing when imparted to other people.

In the domain of body change, the narratives of weight reduction ventures hold a noticeable spot. These accounts frequently dive into the intricacies of the connection among people and their bodies. Examples of overcoming adversity in weight reduction investigate the actual changes as well as the profound and mental movements that go with shedding overabundance weight. The freshly discovered identity regard, certainty, and further developed in general prosperity turns into a demonstration of the significant effect of weight reduction on both body and psyche.

Likewise, accounts of muscle gain and working out exhibit the extraordinary force of solidarity preparing and opposition work out. People who set out on excursions to assemble muscle frequently share the commitment expected to shape their constitutions. These examples of overcoming adversity commend the versatility expected to push through testing exercises, stick to restrained preparing regimens, and make the fundamental way of life acclimations to help muscle development.

As opposed to accounts revolved around weight reduction or muscle gain, examples of overcoming adversity in body change likewise incorporate those zeroed in on by and large wellbeing and prosperity. These accounts feature people who focus on health as an all encompassing idea, consolidating propensities that advance mental lucidity, profound equilibrium, and a feeling of satisfaction. The accentuation isn't exclusively on outside appearances however on developing a manageable and lively condition of wellbeing.

The festival of examples of overcoming adversity in body and life change stretches out past actual achievements to envelop psychological well-being ventures. Accounts of people defeating difficulties like tension, despondency, or self-perception issues show the significant effect of mental prosperity on in general change. These stories stress the significance of looking for proficient help, rehearsing self-empathy, and taking on ways of dealing with especially difficult times that add to a positive mental state.

The crossing point of innovation and body change is a critical part of contemporary examples of overcoming adversity. With the approach of wellness applications, wearables, and online networks, people have phenomenal admittance to assets that help their excursions. Examples of overcoming adversity frequently highlight the coordination of innovation, displaying how people influence computerized instruments to follow progress, access virtual exercises, and interface with similar networks.

As we celebrate examples of overcoming adversity of body and life change, it is fundamental to perceive the variety of ways people take to accomplish their objectives. The stories incorporate a large number of ages, foundations, and beginning stages. Every story is a one of a kind demonstration of the singular's organization, featuring that change is a profoundly private excursion molded by one's own desires and conditions.

The far reaching influence of these examples of overcoming adversity stretches out past the actual people, impacting networks and rousing others to leave on their own extraordinary excursions. The stories become encouraging signs, separating generalizations, and testing cultural standards encompassing excellence, wellbeing, and prosperity. The festival of different examples of overcoming adversity adds to a more comprehensive and enabling story around body change.

9.2 Emphasizing the ongoing nature of personal development and fitness

Chasing self-improvement and wellness, the excursion is definitely not a limited objective yet rather a nonstop, developing interaction. The acknowledgment of self-improvement as a continuous undertaking highlights the unique idea of human life, where variation, learning, and improvement are constants. This story means to dive into the multi-layered parts of self-improvement and wellness, underlining the meaning of embracing the excursion as a long lasting responsibility.

At the center of self-improvement lies the comprehension that people are never-ending works underway. The continuous idea of self-improvement infers a guarantee to self-disclosure, reflection, and deliberate development. This excursion unfurls through different phases of life, adjusting to the changing scenes of encounters, difficulties, and open doors. A story urges people to see self-awareness not as a progression of secluded objectives but rather as a comprehensive, deep rooted process.

The obligation to progressing self-improvement includes developing a development outlook — a conviction that one's capacities and knowledge can be created through commitment and difficult work. This mentality cultivates versatility even with difficulties, empowering people to consider mishaps to be open doors for learning and improvement. The continuous idea of self-awareness is obvious in the versatility to adjust to new conditions, procure new abilities, and explore the intricacies of existence with a consistent eagerness to learn.

In the domain of individual wellness, an equal excursion unfurls — one that lines up with the continuous idea of self-awareness. Wellness is certainly not a static accomplishment yet a powerful condition of prosperity that incorporates physical, mental, and close to home aspects. The obligation to wellness as a continuous pursuit requires a change in context, creating some distance from transient objectives towards a way of life that focuses on reasonable wellbeing and essentialness.

The continuous idea of individual wellness includes a comprehensive methodology that reaches out past inconsistent exercises or transitory dietary changes. It envelops a guarantee to ordinary active work, adjusted sustenance, and mental prosperity as vital parts of a sound way of life. This approach perceives that ideal wellness is a finish of predictable propensities supported over the long haul, as opposed to a handy solution or an impermanent arrangement.

Actual wellness, in its continuous interest, turns into an impression of by and large prosperity. The story of continuous individual wellness recognizes that the body is a unique living being, receptive to improves on in propensities, sustenance, and way of life. An excursion commends the variety of wellness modalities, perceiving that people might find euphoria and maintainability in exercises going from conventional exercises to yoga, climbing, or group activities.

The continuous obligation to individual wellness likewise includes adjusting to the changing requirements of the body across various life stages. Similarly as self-awareness advances, so does the relationship with one's actual wellbeing. The story of continuous wellness recognizes that needs, objectives, and actual limits might move over the long run, requiring adaptability in one's way to deal with keep a comprehensive feeling of prosperity.

Mental and close to home prosperity are basic aspects of progressing individual wellness. The interconnected idea of psyche and body features the significance of psychological wellness chasing actual wellness.

The continuous story of individual wellness perceives the job of pressure the executives, care, and profound strength as fundamental parts of an all encompassing prosperity venture.

In the story of progressing self-improvement and wellness, the idea of self-sympathy arises as a core value. Recognizing that difficulties, difficulties, and vacillations are inborn in any excursion, self-empathy urges people to treat themselves with graciousness and understanding. The continuous obligation to self-improvement and wellness isn't about flawlessness however about progress, perceiving that each forward-moving step is a triumph, regardless of the speed.

The cultural account around self-improvement and wellness frequently underscores quick changes, moment results, and the quest for outer beliefs. Nonetheless, the continuous idea of self-improvement challenges this account, asking people to focus on feasible development over handy solutions. It welcomes a shift from outer approval to characteristic inspiration, where the delight of the excursion turns into a main impetus, and the objective is perceived as a ceaseless course of becoming.

Schooling and mindfulness assume urgent parts in encouraging the continuous account of self-awareness and wellness. Engaging people with the information on the body's many-sided components, the advantages of a reasonable way of life, and the mental parts of prosperity develops an establishment for informed direction. The continuous quest for information turns into an impetus for economical propensities and informed decisions that line up with long haul wellbeing and self-improvement.

The incorporation of innovation additionally adds to the continuous story of self-awareness and wellness. In the computerized age, people approach a heap of devices, applications, and stages that work with picking up, following advancement, and interfacing with similar networks. The continuous idea of self-awareness is upheld by innovation that enables people to lay out objectives, screen their excursion, and access assets that line up with their novel ways.

The continuous account of self-improvement and wellness crosses with the idea of work-life coordination. In our current reality where expert and individual circles are progressively interconnected, the quest for self-awareness and wellness turns into an essential part of a healthy lifestyle. The continuous obligation to development stretches out past conventional limits, recognizing that self-improvement and wellness are fundamental parts of a satisfying and balanced presence.

The work environment, as a critical setting for self-improvement, can add to the continuous story of development. Associations that focus on worker prosperity, give potential open doors to expertise improvement, and encourage a culture of constant learning add to the continuous excursion of self-improvement. The acknowledgment that people are not static elements but rather advancing supporters of the working environment story lines up with the ethos of continuous self-improvement.

In the cultural story, the festival of assorted ventures becomes essential to underlining the continuous idea of self-improvement and wellness. Every individual's way is extraordinary, molded by private qualities, social impacts, and educational encounters. The continuous story energizes a festival of variety, perceiving that self-awareness and wellness manifest in different structures, and the lavishness of the excursion lies in its uniqueness.

As we investigate the continuous idea of self-awareness and wellness, the significance of objective setting and deliberateness arises as core values. While the excursion is ceaseless, setting clear aims and explicit, sensible objectives gives guidance and inspiration. The continuous story includes intermittent reflection, change of objectives, and the acknowledgment that the quest for development is a purposeful, deliberate decision.

Individual connections and social associations assume a fundamental part in the continuous story of self-awareness and wellness. The help and support of companions, family, or local area add to the flexibility expected to explore difficulties and celebrate triumphs. The interconnected idea of self-awareness underscores the public perspective, recognizing that the continuous excursion is enhanced when imparted to other people.

The continuous account of self-awareness and wellness rises above age, recognizing that the excursion is significant across the life expectancy. Whether in youth, adulthood, or the senior years, people keep on developing, learn, and adjust. The continuous obligation to development turns into a deep rooted buddy, directing people through the various times of existence with strength and a feeling of direction.

9.3 Encouraging readers to continue refining both their iron will and steel physique

In the fantastic orchestra of life, where the tunes of challenge blend with the rhythms of versatility, the quest for a refined and tough reality turns into a long lasting excursion. This story tries to urge perusers to embrace the continuous refinement of both their iron will and steel constitution — a many-sided dance between mental guts and actual strength. It is a challenge to perceive that the excursion of personal development is unending, a ceaseless advancement that requires devotion, flexibility, and a faithful obligation to development.

At the center of this story lies the illustration of the iron will — an image of mental strength, assurance, and the persistence to endure the flames of misfortune. Comparably iron, when manufactured in the pot of difficulties, changes into a substance of solidarity, the human will, when tempered by life's preliminaries, turns into a dauntless power equipped for molding fates. The continuous refinement of the iron will is an acknowledgment that psychological versatility is definitely not a static characteristic however a developing quality that extends with each hardship.

The iron will tracks down its partner in the illustration of the steel body — a portrayal of actual strength, essentialness, and the epitome of restrained exertion. Like steel, which acquires its solidarity through a careful course of manufacturing and forming, the human body develops through reliable preparation, sound propensities, and a pledge to actual prosperity. The continuous refinement of the steel constitution highlights the powerful idea of wellness — an excursion that stretches out past transitory objectives to a supported obligation to wellbeing and imperativeness.

The account of refining the iron will and steel constitution perceives that these two components are reliant, each affecting and improving the other. A versatile brain upholds actual discipline, and a solid build adds to mental grit. The continuous excursion is an all encompassing pursuit that winds around together the strings of mental and actual prosperity, recognizing that genuine strength emerges from the agreeable equilibrium of both.

Fundamental to the continuous refinement of the iron will is the development of mental strength. Life is packed with difficulties, mishaps, and startling turns, and the capacity to explore these with a versatile mentality becomes central. The continuous excursion of mental flexibility includes recognizing mishaps as any open doors for development, keeping up with viewpoint notwithstanding misfortune, and creating survival techniques that support profound prosperity.

The continuous refinement of mental strength is an encouragement to embrace a development outlook — a faith in the limit with regards to constant learning, variation, and improvement. Challenges are not seen as impossible snags but rather as venturing stones on the way to self-awareness. The account urges perusers to move toward misfortunes with interest, perceiving the potential for self-disclosure and the procurement of new abilities all the while.

The continuous excursion of mental versatility likewise includes the act of care — a conscious familiarity with the current second. Care develops a capacity to answer nicely to life's difficulties as opposed to respond hastily. It turns into a device for overseeing pressure, improving concentration, and encouraging a feeling of quiet in the midst of the tempests of life. The continuous refinement of the iron will envelops the ceaseless act of care as an establishment for supported mental strength.

Supplementing the psychological flexibility of the iron will is the continuous obligation to refining the steel body — an excursion of actual prosperity that reaches out past the quest for outer style to the development of all encompassing wellbeing. The story underlines that actual wellness isn't an objective however a continuous cycle that requires consistency, flexibility, and a comprehensive way to deal with prosperity.

The continuous refinement of the steel body includes standard active work as a foundation of a sound way of life.

Whether through organized exercises, sporting exercises, or day to day development, the account urges perusers to track down bliss during the time spent moving their bodies. Active work turns into a festival of the body's capacities, cultivating a positive relationship with development that rises above the bounds of ordinary activity.

Nourishment arises as one more vital part of the continuous refinement of the steel physical make-up. The story advocates for a fair and manageable way to deal with sustenance — one that supports the body with healthy, supplement thick food varieties. The continuous excursion includes a comprehension of individual dietary requirements, careful dietary patterns, and an acknowledgment that sustenance is an essential part of in general prosperity.

Rest and recuperation are essential parts of the continuous story of actual prosperity. The story urges perusers to see the value in the significance of sufficient rest, rest days, and stress the board chasing a strong and solid build. The continuous refinement of the steel build recognizes that genuine strength isn't just worked through effort yet additionally through the supportive cycles that happen during times of rest.

The continuous excursion of actual prosperity is likewise set apart by versatility — an acknowledgment that the body's necessities might develop with time, conditions, and age. The story urges perusers to be receptive to their bodies, changing their wellness schedules, nourishment, and taking care of oneself practices in light of evolving needs. The continuous refinement of the steel body is a powerful interaction that embraces flexibility as a vital component of supported prosperity.

Mind-body association is a focal topic in the continuous story of refining both the iron will and steel constitution. The affirmation that psychological and actual prosperity are interconnected highlights the all encompassing nature of self-improvement. The account urges perusers to investigate rehearses that improve the brain body association, like yoga, contemplation, or careful development. The continuous refinement includes developing a familiarity with what mental states mean for actual prosperity as well as the other way around.

Chasing refining both the iron will and steel build, the job of local area and backing arises as a huge variable. The story underscores the force of shared encounters, common support, and a feeling of having a place in cultivating progressing development. Whether through exercise accomplices, wellness networks, or steady informal communities, the continuous excursion becomes advanced when imparted to other people who rouse, spur, and add to the aggregate flexibility and strength.

Innovation turns into a partner in the continuous account of self-awareness and wellness. In the computerized age, people approach an abundance of assets that work with their excursions.

Wellness applications, wearable gadgets, and online networks give apparatuses to following advancement, getting to exercises, and interfacing with similar people. The continuous refinement of both the iron will and steel build is upheld by innovation that enables people to put forth and accomplish customized objectives.

Celebrating progress turns into a fundamental part of the continuous story. The story urges perusers to recognize and praise their accomplishments, regardless of how little, perceiving that each forward-moving step is a demonstration of their responsibility and versatility. The continuous refinement isn't exclusively about arriving at stupendous achievements however valuing the gradual advancement and the actual excursion.

As perusers leave on the continuous excursion of refining both their iron will and steel physical make-up, the story turns into a wellspring of motivation and inspiration. It is a call to embrace the unique idea of self-awareness — an excursion that rises above brief objectives and on second thought centers around the ceaseless course of becoming. The continuous story is an update that the quest for a refined and versatile presence isn't an objective however a deep rooted responsibility — one that requires commitment, flexibility, and an unflinching faith in the continuous potential for development.

In the ensemble of personal development, the transaction between an iron will and a steel body addresses a unique concordance of mental grit and actual strength. This story looks to dig into the complicated connection between the two, perceiving that the refinement of both the iron will and steel physical make-up is definitely not a static accomplishment yet a continuous, deep rooted process.

The illustration of an iron will invokes pictures of steadfast assurance, versatility, and an unyielding soul. It represents the psychological strength expected to explore the difficulties of life, to endure affliction, and to continue on chasing after objectives. The continuous refinement of the iron will is an acknowledgment that psychological versatility is certainly not a decent characteristic yet a quality that develops and develops with each insight.

At the core of the iron will is the capacity to confront misfortunes and disappointments with a mentality that sees them not as impossible hindrances, but rather as venturing stones on the way to self-awareness. The continuous excursion of mental versatility includes the development of a development outlook — a confidence in the potential for ceaseless learning, variation, and improvement. Challenges are embraced as any open doors for self-disclosure and the procurement of new abilities, supporting the account that mishaps are not endpoints but rather impetuses for progress.

Care arises as a vital part in the continuous refinement of the iron will. The purposeful act of being available at the time develops a mindfulness that rises above the tumult of outer conditions.

Care turns into an instrument for overseeing pressure, keeping up with viewpoint, and cultivating a feeling of quiet in the midst of the tempests of life. The continuous excursion of the iron will incorporates the nonstop act of care as an establishment for supported mental strength.

Supplementing the figurative iron will is the idea of the steel constitution — a portrayal of actual strength, versatility, and the encapsulation of trained exertion. Like steel, which acquires its solidarity through a fastidious course of producing and forming, the human build develops through predictable preparation, sound propensities, and a pledge to actual prosperity. The continuous refinement of the steel constitution is an acknowledgment that actual wellness isn't an objective yet a consistent excursion that requires devotion and a comprehensive way to deal with prosperity.

The continuous refinement of the steel build includes customary active work as a foundation of a sound way of life. Development turns into a festival of the body's capacities, encouraging a positive relationship that rises above the bounds of traditional activity. Whether through organized exercises, sporting exercises, or day to day development, the story urges people to track down bliss during the time spent moving their bodies.

Nourishment arises as one more vital part of the continuous refinement of the steel body. The story advocates for a decent and economical way to deal with sustenance — one that supports the body with healthy, supplement thick food varieties. The continuous excursion includes a comprehension of individual dietary requirements, careful dietary patterns, and an acknowledgment that sustenance is a crucial part of by and large prosperity.

Rest and recuperation are indispensable parts of the continuous account of actual prosperity. The story urges people to see the value in the significance of sufficient rest, rest days, and stress the board chasing a strong and sound build. The continuous refinement of the steel build recognizes that genuine strength isn't just worked through effort yet in addition through the supportive cycles that happen during times of rest.

Versatility turns into an essential topic in the continuous excursion of refining both the iron will and steel physical make-up. The story perceives that the body's requirements might advance with time, conditions, and age. People are urged to be sensitive to their bodies, changing their wellness schedules, sustenance, and taking care of oneself practices in light of evolving needs. The continuous refinement turns into a powerful interaction that embraces flexibility as a vital component of supported prosperity.

Mind-body association is a focal subject in the continuous story of refining both the iron will and steel physical make-up. The affirmation that psychological and actual prosperity are interconnected highlights the all encompassing nature of self-improvement.

The story urges people to investigate rehearses that improve the brain body association, like yoga, reflection, or careful development. The continuous refinement includes developing a consciousness of what mental states mean for actual prosperity as well as the other way around.

Chasing refining both the iron will and steel build, the job of local area and backing arises as a huge component. The story stresses the force of shared encounters, common support, and a feeling of having a place in cultivating progressing development. Whether through exercise accomplices, wellness networks, or strong informal communities, the continuous excursion becomes advanced when imparted to other people who rouse, persuade, and add to the aggregate versatility and strength.

Innovation turns into a partner in the continuous account of self-improvement and wellness. In the computerized age, people approach an abundance of assets that work with their excursions. Wellness applications, wearable gadgets, and online networks give apparatuses to following advancement, getting to exercises, and associating with similar people. The continuous refinement of both the iron will and steel constitution is upheld by innovation that enables people to define and accomplish customized objectives.

Celebrating progress turns into an indispensable part of the continuous story. The story urges people to recognize and commend their accomplishments, regardless of how little, perceiving that each step in the right direction is a demonstration of their responsibility and versatility. The continuous refinement isn't exclusively about arriving at great achievements yet valuing the steady advancement and the actual excursion.

As people leave on the continuous excursion of refining both their iron will and steel constitution, the story turns into a wellspring of motivation and inspiration. It is a call to embrace the powerful idea of self-improvement — an excursion that rises above brief objectives and on second thought centers around the constant course of becoming. The continuous story is an update that the quest for a refined and strong presence isn't an objective however a long lasting responsibility — one that requires devotion, versatility, and an unfaltering faith in the continuous potential for development.

www.ingramcontent.com/pod-product-compliance
Lightning Source LLC
LaVergne TN
LVHW010218070526
838199LV00062B/4647